Copyright on the Internet
ILLUSTRATED

ESSENTIALS

Barbara M. Waxer / Marsha L. Baum

THOMSON
COURSE TECHNOLOGY

Australia • Canada • Mexico • Singapore • Spain • United Kingdom • United States

THOMSON

COURSE TECHNOLOGY

Copyright on the Internet—Illustrated Essentials
Waxer/Baum

Senior Acquisitions Editor:
Marjorie Hunt

Product Manager:
Jennifer Muroff

Associate Product Manager:
Janine Tangney

Editorial Assistant:
Rebecca Padrick

Development Editor:
MT Cozzola

Senior Content Project Manager:
Philippa Lehar

Copy Editor:
Karen Annett

Proofreader:
Kathy Orrino

Indexer:
Rich Carlson

Senior Marketing Manager:
Joy Stark

Marketing Coordinator:
Melissa Marcoux

Interior Designer:
Stephanie Fall

Cover Designer:
Steve Deschene

Composition:
GEX Publishing Services

Author Acknowledgements

Thanks to Senior Acquisitions Editor Marjorie Hunt for expanding the audience for copyright-related issues. Her vision helps promote an informed and literate student community. Project Manager Jen Muroff guided us perfectly in meeting an ambitious deadline.

Having the multi-talented MT Cozzola as a Development Editor gave this project much-needed perspective and always makes it a great ride. Exalted superlatives can't even come close to describing her contributions or her humor.

Thanks to Production Editor Philippa Lehar for effortlessly assembling ever-increasing parts and pieces and to GEX for their creativity in the concept art. Special kudos to Heather Scherer, Heather Lind and Gifford Scanlon. Many thanks also to our copy editor, Karen Annett, and proofreader, Kathy Orrino, for catching the fallout, and to our reviewers, Ken Wade, Champlain College and Leah Noonan, Laramie County Community College for their detailed reviews and feedback. Senior Marketing Manager Joy Stark deserves much credit for great nuanced work and educating our sales force so they can better serve their instructors.

I am indebted to Marsha Baum for her commitment to educating students, artists, and everyone in the workforce about copyright law. She has always been extraordinarily patient and entertaining when conveying the finer points of intellectual property law to me, her most difficult student. Thanks always to my partner, Lindy, for putting up with it all.
— Barbara M. Waxer

With great appreciation to Barbara Waxer for her vision, her wit, and her exceptional willingness to include others in her work. Thank you to the University of New Mexico School of Law administration, particularly Dean Suellyn Scarnecchia, for providing research support for projects such as this. And, a special thank you to my husband Richard for proving the value of a good partner and for his unfailing encouragement and exceptional care of our two-year-old daughters, Amanda and Elise Klingler.
— Marsha L. Baum

Legal Disclaimer

This book concentrates on copyright law and, tangentially, trademark law as the two types of intellectual property law that will have the most impact on Web designers, artists, and anyone using Internet images and media. This book does not provide legal advice and use of this book does not establish an attorney-client relationship. It provides an overview of the law and offers examples, but does not provide comprehensive coverage on the nuances of copyright or trademark law. For specific legal questions and concerns, consult your lawyer.

Preface

Welcome to *Copyright on the Internet—Illustrated Essentials*! Copyright infringement is a hot topic for both new and seasoned computer and Internet users. Copyright affects us every day, throughout the day. This book will help you to expand your knowledge by becoming more proficient in the language, purpose, and application of copyright in your educational and work environments. Wielding a rudimentary understanding of how copyright works, the issues surrounding entertainment media, and how to use protected work properly is essential for a productive—and legal—experience when handling any media file.

This book bridges the gap between creators and users of Internet media and the legal constructs under which they must operate.

Designed for All Users

The modular approach and the unique page layout of this book make it an appropriate learning tool for both the novice and the experienced user. Each lesson focuses on a relevant concept and is presented on two facing pages so that you don't have to turn the page to find an illustration or finish a paragraph. Also, because the text is organized in a modular fashion, you can choose to read all the lesson material or only those paragraphs where you need to "fill in the gaps."

A single concept is presented in a two-page "information display" to help you absorb information quickly and easily

Easy-to-follow introductions to every lesson focus on a single concept to help you get the information quickly

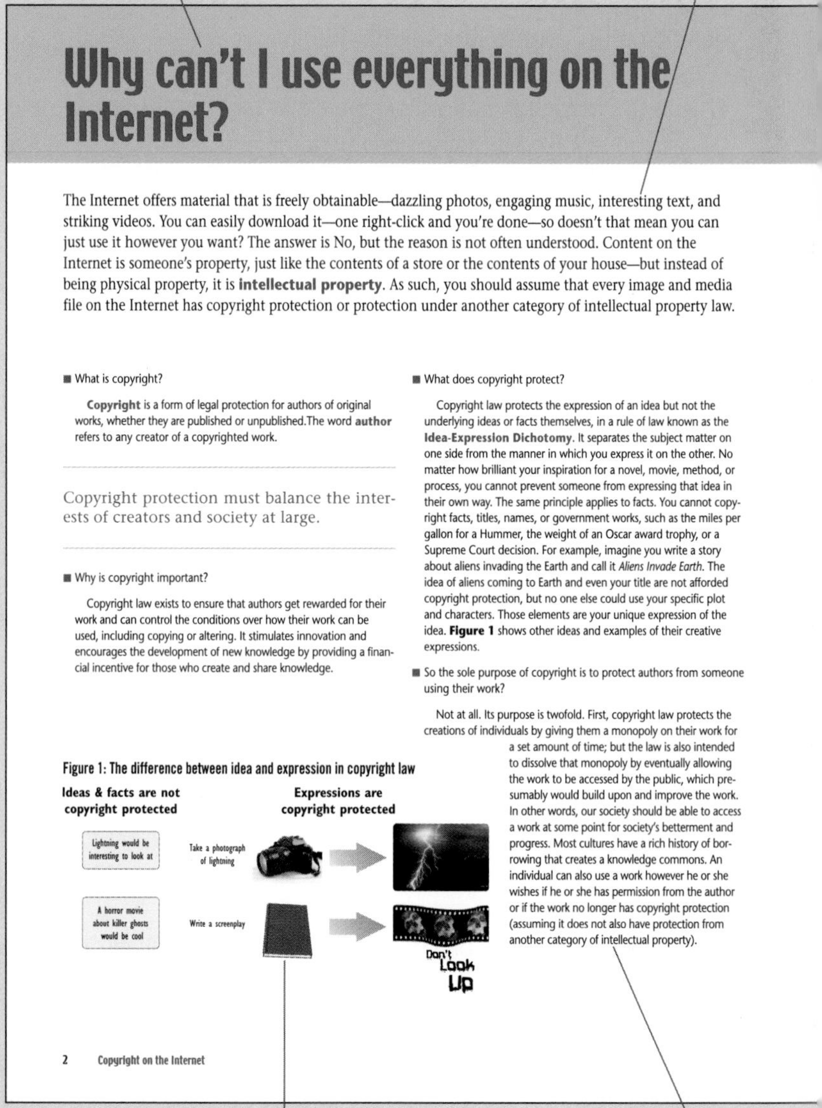

Why can't I use everything on the Internet?

The Internet offers material that is freely obtainable—dazzling photos, engaging music, interesting text, and striking videos. You can easily download it—one right-click and you're done—so doesn't that mean you can just use it however you want? The answer is No, but the reason is not often understood. Content on the Internet is someone's property, just like the contents of a store or the contents of your house—but instead of being physical property, it is **intellectual property**. As such, you should assume that every image and media file on the Internet has copyright protection or protection under another category of intellectual property law.

■ What is copyright?

Copyright is a form of legal protection for authors of original works, whether they are published or unpublished. The word **author** refers to any creator of a copyrighted work.

Copyright protection must balance the interests of creators and society at large.

■ Why is copyright important?

Copyright law exists to ensure that authors get rewarded for their work and can control the conditions over how their work can be used, including copying or altering. It stimulates innovation and encourages the development of new knowledge by providing a financial incentive for those who create and share knowledge.

■ What does copyright protect?

Copyright law protects the expression of an idea but not the underlying ideas or facts themselves, in a rule of law known as the **Idea-Expression Dichotomy**. It separates the subject matter on one side from the manner in which you express it on the other. No matter how brilliant your inspiration for a novel, movie, method, or process, you cannot prevent someone from expressing that idea in their own way. The same principle applies to facts. You cannot copyright facts, titles, names, or government works, such as the miles per gallon for a Hummer, the weight of an Oscar award trophy, or a Supreme Court decision. For example, imagine you write a story about aliens invading the Earth and call it *Aliens Invade Earth*. The idea of aliens coming to Earth and even your title are not afforded copyright protection, but no one else could use your specific plot and characters. Those elements are your unique expression of the idea. **Figure 1** shows other ideas and examples of their creative expressions.

■ So the sole purpose of copyright is to protect authors from someone using their work?

Not at all. Its purpose is twofold. First, copyright law protects the creations of individuals by giving them a monopoly on their work for a set amount of time; but the law is also intended to dissolve that monopoly by eventually allowing the work to be accessed by the public, which presumably would build upon and improve the work. In other words, our society should be able to access a work at some point for society's betterment and progress. Most cultures have a rich history of borrowing that creates a knowledge commons. An individual can also use a work however he or she wishes if he or she has permission from the author or if the work no longer has copyright protection (assuming it does not also have protection from another category of intellectual property).

Figure 1: The difference between idea and expression in copyright law

Ideas & facts are not copyright protected

Lightning would be interesting to look at

A horror movie about killer ghosts would be cool

Expressions are copyright protected

Take a photograph of lightning

Write a screenplay

Don't Look Up

Large photos, screenshots, and drawings are integrated into the text to better illustrate the lesson concepts

Modular text allows you to jump to sections to cover exactly what you need to learn

Up-to-Date Information

Technology and the law move quickly, and we have made sure to include the most current information in this book. You will learn about the latest issues in copyright law as they specifically pertain to media you can upload to and download from the Internet. The intersection of the law and the Internet can easily create conflict, and can change as the courts align the law to new technologies and as schools and businesses adjust to new issues and possibilities.

Online Companion Web Site

There are literally thousands of sites that invite visitors to use text, sound, music, graphics, photos, or video. Finding them is another matter. The *Online Companion* Web site features a comprehensive online resource filled with listings of sites that offer public domain or open access files.

FYIs provide pertinent user information or additional background information on the lesson concept

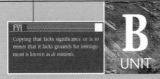

FYI

Copying that lacks significance or is so minor that it lacks grounds for infringement is known as *de minimis*.

B
UNIT

■ What is the difference between theft, copyright infringement, and plagiarism?

Many of us think of theft as meaning any illegal appropriation of someone else's property. Thus, posting a copyrighted photograph of a Mustang on a Web site, stealing a Mustang GT from someone's driveway, and copying the song "Mustang Sally" can all be seen as examples of theft. In the legal landscape, stealing physical items is called theft and is punishable under criminal law; "stealing" or "pirating" copyrighted works is infringement of the rights of the copyright owner, and is punishable under civil law. **Plagiarism** occurs when you quote an amount of a *written* work and do not attribute the words to the author. The problem is not that you're quoting text, it's

that you are not providing credit by attributing the work to the author. Although plagiarism is generally considered an academic offense (for which students can suffer consequences ranging from a failing grade to outright dismissal), it is not punishable under civil law; however, it can easily morph into infringement when you use extensive or substantial amounts of the work.

It is important to understand that attribution, although a great standard practice, is *never* a defense against infringement. In other words, giving credit to the copyright holder of a song or photo indicates that you are not trying to claim the work as your own, but it doesn't mean you are using the work properly, with permission. **Figure 21** compares the differences between plagiarism and copyright infringement.

Figure 21: Comparing plagiarism and copyright infringement

	PLAGIARISM	INFRINGEMENT
What's affected	Written work	Any work of authorship
Classification	Academic dishonesty	Copyright law violation
Effect	Fools reader into believing you wrote the work	Denies copyright owner reward for creation
Consequence	Failing grade; expulsion; loss of degree, job, or publishing contract	May be liable for damages; can no longer use material
How to avoid consequences	Give proper credit to author or source	Obtain permission from owner to use the work

Understanding legal lingo

In a legal setting, the words infringement and violation have special meaning. In intellectual property, you can *infringe* someone's copyright, patent, or trademark, whereas rights of publicity and privacy are said to be *violated*. And, if you are ever sued and the court finds that you have indeed infringed or

violated, you are *liable*, not guilty. The legal system does not brand you as a pirate, thief, or bandit. It's most important that you understand the concepts behind the laws, regardless of the words you use.

Clues to Use boxes relate the lesson material to real-world situations to provide additional practical information

Instructor Resources

The Instructor Resources CD is Course Technology's way of putting the resources and information needed to teach and learn effectively into instructors' hands. With an integrated array of teaching and learning tools that offer a broad range of technology-based instructional options, we believe this CD represents the highest quality and most cutting edge resources available to instructors today. Many of these resources are available at **www.course.com**.

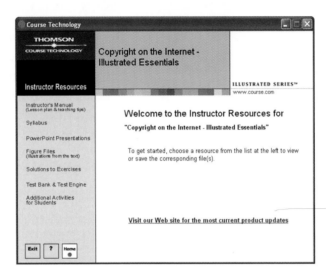

- Figure Files—Includes every image from the book, which can be used to create transparencies or a PowerPoint presentation.

- Solutions to Exercises—Solutions to Exercises contains examples of the work students are asked to create in the End-of-Unit material and Independent Challenges.

- **Test Bank & Test Engine**—ExamView is a powerful testing software package that allows instructors to create and administer printed, computer (LAN-based), and Internet exams. ExamView includes hundreds of questions that correspond to the topics covered in this text, enabling students to generate detailed study guides that include page references for further review. The computer-based and Internet testing components allow students to take exams at their computers, and also saves you time by grading each exam automatically.

- Instructor's Manual—Available as an electronic file, the Instructor's Manual is quality-assurance tested and includes a Lecture Note for every lesson, Teaching Tips, Quick Quizzes, and Classroom Activities.

- Syllabus—Instructors can prepare their course easily using this sample outline.

- PowerPoint Presentations—Each unit has a corresponding PowerPoint presentation that can be used in lecture, distributed to students, or customized.

Credits

Contents

UNIT A

Why Copyright Matters   1

UNIT B

Unauthorized Use and Fair Use   25

Why Copyright Matters

Why can't I use everything on the Internet?
When does copyright protection begin?
What exactly does a copyright holder own?
What happens to copyright when I buy work?
How do I protect my own work?
What work is not copyright protected?
How do I find media I can use?

Topics and Inquiries: Artistic expression or illegal acquisition?
Copyright in Context: Determining use

Overview

This unit provides an overview of copyright protection—what it is, how you get it, and what your rights are after you have it. Specifically, you learn why although media files and text are publicly available on the Internet, they are not necessarily free to use at will. You will also discover the specifics of copyright protection, the types of work that are afforded protection, and the rights you have as a copyright holder. You also gain an understanding of what it means for a work to be in the public domain and how to find works you can use in your own projects.

Why can't I use everything on the Internet?

The Internet offers material that is freely obtainable—dazzling photos, engaging music, interesting text, and striking videos. You can easily download it—one right-click and you're done—so doesn't that mean you can just use it however you want? The answer is No, but the reason is not often understood. Content on the Internet is someone's property, just like the contents of a store or the contents of your house—but instead of being physical property, it is **intellectual property**. As such, you should assume that every image and media file on the Internet has copyright protection or protection under another category of intellectual property law.

■ What is copyright?

Copyright is a form of legal protection for authors of original works, whether they are published or unpublished. The word **author** refers to any creator of a copyrighted work.

Copyright protection must balance the interests of creators and society at large.

■ Why is copyright important?

Copyright law exists to ensure that authors get rewarded for their work and can control the conditions over how their work can be used, including copying or altering. It stimulates innovation and encourages the development of new knowledge by providing a financial incentive for those who create and share knowledge.

■ What does copyright protect?

Copyright law protects the expression of an idea but not the underlying ideas or facts themselves, in a rule of law known as the **Idea-Expression Dichotomy**. It separates the subject matter on one side from the manner in which you express it on the other. No matter how brilliant your inspiration for a novel, movie, method, or process, you cannot prevent someone from expressing that idea in their own way. The same principle applies to facts. You cannot copyright facts, titles, names, or government works, such as the miles per gallon for a Hummer, the weight of an Oscar award trophy, or a Supreme Court decision. For example, imagine you write a story about aliens invading the Earth and call it *Aliens Invade Earth*. The idea of aliens coming to Earth and even your title are not afforded copyright protection, but no one else could use your specific plot and characters. Those elements are your unique expression of the idea. **Figure 1** shows other ideas and examples of their creative expressions.

■ So the sole purpose of copyright is to protect authors from someone using their work?

Not at all. Its purpose is twofold. First, copyright law protects the creations of individuals by giving them a monopoly on their work for

Figure 1: The difference between idea and expression in copyright law

Ideas & facts are not copyright protected		Expressions are copyright protected
Lightning would be interesting to look at	Take a photograph of lightning	
A horror movie about killer ghosts would be cool	Write a screenplay	Don't Look Up

a set amount of time; but the law is also intended to dissolve that monopoly by eventually allowing the work to be accessed by the public, which presumably would build upon and improve the work. In other words, our society should be able to access a work at some point for society's betterment and progress. Most cultures have a rich history of borrowing that creates a knowledge commons. An individual can also use a work however he or she wishes if he or she has permission from the author or if the work no longer has copyright protection (assuming it does not also have protection from another category of intellectual property).

■ Why is it important to balance protection and innovation?

More than any other type of intellectual property, copyright protection must balance the interests of creators and society at large. On one hand, protecting copyright encourages individuals to create and innovate; on the other hand, when society has access to these creations, that access also stimulates innovation. **Figure 2** illustrates the cycle of progress that makes copyright protection so complicated. Copyright law has changed in response to technological advancements;

technology creates new material eligible for copyright protection and users apply technology to infringe copyright. For example, two hundred years ago, no one imagined photography or recorded music; one hundred years ago, few imagined nationwide electricity, radio, or phone service; and fifty years ago, few imagined the impact of computer hardware, software, and portable electronics.

■ What are the issues?

■ Copyright owners are concerned that their right to their work is at risk and that new technologies, such as file-sharing software, make it increasingly easier to violate copyright by "stealing" material. Access to and use of a work will affect revenue streams and, it is argued, ultimately limit the availability of creative works because creators would no longer be motivated to create.

■ Users of copyrighted work and the public are concerned that society's ability to use materials under existing copyright exemptions will be eroded, and that a millennia-old tradition of creating, borrowing, innovating, and improving will be lost.

Figure 2: Achieving balance between copyright law and technology is a constant challenge

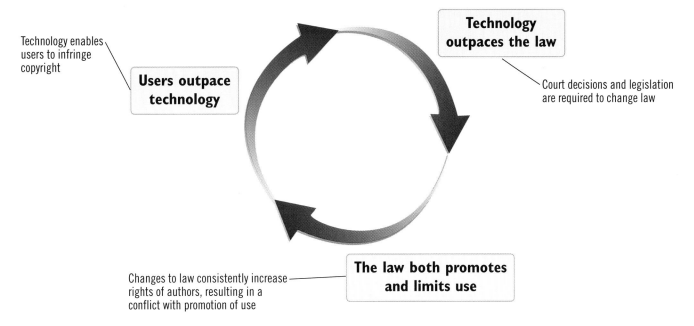

Technology enables users to infringe copyright

Users outpace technology

Technology outpaces the law

Court decisions and legislation are required to change law

Changes to law consistently increase rights of authors, resulting in a conflict with promotion of use

The law both promotes and limits use

Understanding intellectual property

Copyright law is a category of intellectual property law, which establishes how and when a person and society as a whole can benefit and profit from someone's intellectual creation. We are surrounded by elements of intellectual property 24 hours a day. Intellectual property is a product resulting from some sort of human creativity. It can include inventions, movies, songs, designs, architecture, logos, clothing—anything created through intellectual or mental labor. Unlike real property (better known as real estate), or personal property (better known as your stuff), it is referred to as an intangible asset because it is created through intellectual or mental labor. In other words, a CD itself is not intellectual property, but the songs on the CD are.

When does copyright protection begin?

As you learned earlier in this unit, copyright protects the expression of an idea, though not the idea or fact that inspired the expression. This lesson explains the concepts necessary for understanding how and when copyright attaches to work.

■ How does my work obtain copyright protection?

Once you create an original work, you don't have to do anything to obtain copyright protection for it. You don't have to publish your work, and you don't have to register it. Copyright protects your original work of authorship fixed in any tangible medium of expression, as soon as it is captured in a physical form.

Copyright protects your original work...as soon as it is captured in a physical form.

■ And that means...?

To fully understand this concept, you need to understand a few legal terms:

The work must be **original**—that is, a product of the creator, although not necessarily novel or unique. It can be similar to existing works (such as two people photographing the same scene) and it can be absolutely devoid of ingenuity, quality, or artistic value. This includes work such as a Pulitzer prize-winning photo, the winner of a Webby Web design award, the winners of a Worst Song Ever Written contest, and your handmade Halloween costume of your favorite fruit or vegetable. The work must reflect some amount of creative effort, however minimal.

■ A **work of authorship** includes many forms, including those not yet realized by new technologies.

• Literary works, such as books, poetry, plays, compilations, and computer programs (including games and Web pages)

• Musical works, including lyrics or any accompanying words

• Dramatic works, including any accompanying music

• Pantomimes and choreographic works

• Pictorial, graphic, and sculptural works, including architectural plans, two- and three-dimensional art, photographs, maps, charts, diagrams, computer graphics, and models

• Motion pictures and other audiovisual works, including scores, speech, and sound effects

• Sound recordings, including music, speech, and sound not covered by motion pictures and audiovisual works

• Architectural works

Figure 3: Conditions for copyright protection

| Action 1 | You compose "Hit Song" | Action 2 | You use a method to fix the work | Action 3 | Protected: the song "Hit Song" |

Record song onto a device

OR

Write or transpose song onto sheet music

- Fixed in a **tangible medium of expression** refers to the form in which a work can be viewed or experienced, for no matter how brief a period of time. To be protected, the work must be able to be observed, reproduced, or communicated. Examples include paper, recordings, video, digital media, or the random access memory (RAM) in a computer. The key word is fixed—talking aloud to your dog about an idea for a movie and later seeing a movie made with a similar plot does not entitle you to claim copyright infringement. But, if you scribbled story details on an envelope or sent a text message (and the recipient kept the message), your expression is protected by copyright because it is fixed. Similarly, your computer fixes a work when you save a graphic. You can claim copyright infringement when someone uses your work without your permission. **Figure 3** shows the dynamic of originality, work of authorship, and tangible medium of expression necessary for a work to acquire copyright.

It used to be that to obtain valid copyright protection you had to register your work with the Copyright Office in the Library of Congress. That's why on works published prior to March 1, 1989, you see the copyright symbol © or the word "Copyright," indicating that it has such protection. Although registration is no longer required, you can still include the © symbol with your work. Registering a work with the Copyright Office does provide a distinct legal advantage if someone infringes your work, which you learn about in a later lesson. Table 1 describes the symbols associated with copyright and other categories of intellectual property.

Table 1: Trademark and Copyright symbols

SYMBOL	TYPE	USE
©	Copyright	Necessary for copyrighted works created prior to 3/1/89; since 1989, optional for all works
℗	Copyright	Work requires a sound recording copyright
®	Trademark	Work is registered with U.S. Patent Office
™	Trademark	Work is not registered with U.S. Patent Office
SM	Service Mark	Work is not registered with U.S. Patent Office

Other categories of intellectual property law

In addition to copyright law, there are several other important branches of intellectual property law.

Patent law protects an invention, process, or method. Generally, the laws of nature are not patentable, but their applications are. So, you could patent a design for a new roller coaster, but not the laws of physics that make it thrilling.

Trademark law protects a distinctive word, symbol, or design that identifies their goods or services. The Ben & Jerry's logo, the Nike swoosh, Mickey Mouse, or the Apple Computer apple are immediately recognizable. Protection related to services is known as a service mark. You can trademark short phrases, terms, and titles, but not copyright them.

Trade secret law protects a secret formula, method, or device, such as the recipe for the Red Bull Energy Drink or the algorithm for Google's search engine.

Trade dress law protects the distinctive appearance of a product or service, such as its packaging size and shape or the color combinations. Examples include décor such as the Outback Steakhouse restaurant chain, or the shape of a Pepperidge Farm Goldfish Cracker.

A design patent protects the ornamental design for an article, but not its function. Examples include the design for Oakley sunglasses, Air Jordan sports shoe, or a Bunn coffee maker.

Right of publicity and right of privacy protect against the use of an individual's likeness for commercial advantage. This right is asserted by celebrities who are in a position to lose financially from the unauthorized use of their identities. The right of privacy protects individuals from interference with their right to be left alone and to protect themselves from unwarranted publicity.

What exactly does a copyright holder own?

When you own copyright to a work, you are granted certain exclusive rights to your work. Generally, it is illegal for someone to do anything with your work that conflicts with these rights. The offending action can be obvious, like outright bootlegging, or it can be more subtle, such as covering a protected song or performing a play in public, even if you don't charge for the performance. There are important legal exceptions, which you learn about in Unit B; for now, you should become familiar with the basics.

■ What are the exclusive rights of copyright owners?

■ As the author of a protected work, you have exclusive rights that control how your work can be used. Collectively, these are known as a "bundle of rights" and consist of the following:

- Reproduction
- Creation of derivative works (for example, a movie version of a book)
- Distribution to the public
- Public performance of literary, musical, dramatic, and choreographic works, pantomimes, and motion pictures and other audiovisual works
- Public display of literary, musical, dramatic, and choreographic works, pantomime, and pictorial, graphic, or sculptural works
- Public performance by digital audio transmission of sound recordings

■ These rights can be broken up at the discretion of the copyright holder. For example, if you took a photograph, you can grant one person the right to publicly display your digital image on a Web site, another person the right to reproduce that image in a magazine, and a third person to use it in a 70-ft. billboard. **Figure 4** traces the bundle of rights associated with a song.

> As the author of a protected work, you have exclusive rights that control how your work can be used.

Figure 4: Bundle of rights afforded to author

■ A closer look at the bundle of rights:

- *Reproduction* involves copying the work, either in whole or in part. Violations include photocopying a book or art, transferring a cartoon or movie character onto a t-shirt, or bootlegging copies of software, music, or video.

- *Derivative works* include transforming or adapting it to any media. For example, the characters from the *Harry Potter* book series are also in films, video games, comics, action figures, and countless other items. Derivative works also include translations, musical arrangements, sound recordings, and subsequent editions of a book.

  - *Sampling music.* Modifying samples from one or more sources qualifies as a derivative work. You cannot capture the value of a song without permission, and the value can be as short as a three-second snippet. For example, the immediacy with which you can recognize the opening notes of Beethoven's Fifth Symphony, the theme of *Jaws* by John Williams, or the introduction to Eric Clapton's "Layla" is evidence of the song's value—and each is less than six seconds in length.

- The right of *distribution to the public* can be by sale, gift, rental, loan, or other transfer.

- *Performing or displaying publicly* occurs in a public place where the majority of people are strangers to you and you transmit or communicate the performance to them, wherever they may be. For example, only you have the right to upload your own short film to your Web site; if someone else uploads it to their Web site, they have violated your right to perform the work. **Figure 5** shows sample scenarios of what represents a public performance.

- *Public performance – digital audio transmission of a sound recording* is a separate public performance right, but only if the performance is a digital audio transmission of the sound recording. Playing a CD on a stereo in the restaurant where you work is not a public performance because you are not transmitting; that is, you are not sending the sounds beyond the stereo. However, if you include songs from the CD in your Internet radio podcast, you do not have a license to play the music; therefore your podcast is considered an unlawful public performance.

Figure 5: What constitutes a public performance?

Public Performance?

Not Prohibited

✓ Singing karaoke at home or entering a contest that uses licensed music

✓ Playing a DVD at home

✓ Recording your favorite TV show and watching it whenever you want

✓ Using your own original music in a podcast

Violation

✗ Creating a karaoke catalog and charging customers to use it

✗ Playing a DVD at a camp or daycare center

✗ Recording your favorite TV show and playing it at your favorite restaurant

✗ Using the current #1 song in a podcast

What happens to copyright when I buy work?

Copyright protection does not last forever, although some would certainly like it to. When you buy a work that has copyright protection, you should understand the distinction between owning the copyright to that work and simply owning a copy of the protected work.

■ How long does copyright protection last?

The general term of protection is the life of the author plus an additional 70 years. So, if you write a song at age 20 in the year 2010, your heirs can continue to benefit from your work for decades, as shown in **Figure 6**. The length of copyright protection has increased considerably over the years. Back in the eighteenth century, the initial term of copyright protection in the United States was 14 years plus a 14-year renewal if the author was still alive. Many other circumstances affect the length of protection, such as publishing date, whether it is a joint work, work for hire, anonymous, or created under an assumed name (known legally as a pseudonymous work).

> When you buy a book, CD, or DVD, you own the physical item, not the copyright inherent in that item.

Figure 6: Typical term of copyright

Term of copyright = Life of author + 70 years

2010	2090	2160
You write "Hit Song"	You die at age 100	70 more years
and make $$	Your heirs begin to earn $$ off of "Hit Song"	Your heirs continue to earn $$ off of "Hit Song"

Total length copyright protection of "Hit Song" is 150 years

■ Don't I own the copyright to a work when I buy the work?

No, a work's copyright status does not change when you buy a copy of the work. When you buy a book, CD, or DVD, you own the physical item, not the copyright inherent in that item. However, the law does allow you to resell, lend, give away, or dispose of that single item. This legal principle is known as the **first sale doctrine**. Because you did not create the work, you do not have any rights that belong to the author, such as making copies and then selling them. This principle also applies to digital content, such as Internet media. Note the first sale doctrine limits the copyright holder's right of distribution, insofar as the purchaser can make personal copies, give the work away, or throw it away.

■ You can make a copy of music or video or tape a television show, but that right is expressly for personal use only. You could also lease or display the work, as do libraries, video and music stores, and museums.

■ Digital technology presents many challenges to copyright law. For example, suppose you buy a mountain bike and later sell it after you've added lights, a cushy seat, an altimeter, and a tire pump; no problem. However, if you buy a computer, load it with popular software, and then sell it still loaded, you've violated the licensing agreement to which you agreed when you initially purchased the software or computer. Let's examine two related examples.

FYI

Selling electronics preloaded with software or media has become a major issue for online shopping sites such as eBay.

A

UNIT

- You want to start a business where you load music onto brand-new iPods (or other MP3 players). Your actions may be legal or illegal, depending on who has purchased the music and who owns the iPod. Generally, you can load music you've legally obtained onto your own iPod. **Figure 7** summarizes the legal status of combining legal and illegal music with your own or someone else's iPod.

- You copy an old music CD to your computer in MP3 format (a process known as **ripping**), then later the computer crashes and you want to rip a newer version of the same CD, but now the CD contains built-in encryption software that prohibits that kind of copying. You have now encountered an area of conflict within the law. On the one hand, you are free to make a copy of your legal purchase for your personal use. However, the Digital Millenium Copyright Act (DMCA) contains provisions that make it a felony to circumvent copyright protection systems. Can you bypass the protection software by claiming that you have a legitimate reason? Court cases point to a mixed verdict, and the law is being vigorously challenged by those who promote use under established legal limitations to copyright protection.

- Other aspects of digital technology make it cumbersome to enjoy personal use of media. For example, iPod owners often experience frustration trying to load and listen to legally purchased songs from a site other than the Apple iTunes Store.

Figure 7: Loading music onto an iPod

Music + = ?

OK	Violation
✓ Load your legally acquired music on your own iPod	✗ Load your legally acquired music on another person's iPod for a fee
✓ Load a friend's legally acquired music on their iPod	✗ Buy iPods, load them with your legally acquired music, and then sell them
✓ Load a customer's legally acquired music on their iPod for a fee	✗ Load illegally acquired music on anyone's device

How do I protect my own work?

Although you might not think twice about downloading work you want to use, the thought of someone using something you created—and possibly profiting from it—might give you pause. Although copyright protection begins as soon as the work is created in a fixed, tangible medium, your strongest legal position is established when you officially register the work.

■ What are the advantages of registering my work?

■ **Registration establishes the work in the public record**. When a work becomes part of the public record, it clearly states the fact that you are the copyright owner.

■ **Registration is necessary before you can file a suit for damages**. Registration is required for you to file a copyright infringement suit against an alleged infringer (although only for works of U.S. origin).

■ **Registration is necessary to be awarded statutory damages and attorneys' fees**. Without registration, you can be awarded actual damages and loss of profits from others using your work for their own financial gain. But, if you register your work within three months after publication of the work or prior to an infringement of the work, you can be awarded statutory damages (damages specifically stated in the law) and attorneys' fees (at the discretion of the court, however).

■ **Registration is necessary to protect against pirated copies**. You can record the registration with the U.S. Customs Service, which protects your work from others importing pirated copies of your work.

■ How do I register my work?

You can download forms at the Copyright Office at the Library of Congress (*www.copyright.gov*). The Copyright Office Web site, shown in **Figure 8**, provides extensive information about copyright law and houses the copyright database. You can register your work at any time before the copyright term expires.

■ Registering your copyright is straightforward: You fill out a short form from the Copyright Office, submit a low fee ($45 at the time of this printing), include copies of the work for deposit, and wait for the reply (which could take several months). The registration becomes effective on the day the Copyright Office receives the package, regardless of when they send out notification.

■ You can download separate forms for literary works, visual arts, performing arts, sound recordings, and serials/periodicals.

For example, **Figure 9** shows a section of the visual arts copyright form.

■ You can also hire a company to register your copyright for you, although they can charge from $70 to $250, including the filing fee.

■ What is a work for hire?

The biggest exception to creator-as-author is when the creator is employed under a work for hire contract. In these cases, the creator is not considered the author of the work and is not entitled to copyright protection. Being hired as a photographer, writer, or graphic artist to create a product is a work for hire arrangement when one of the following requirements is met:

■ The project is a "work prepared by an employee within the scope of his or her employment."

■ The project is a "work specially ordered or commissioned for use," and the contract includes specific language stating that the agreement is work for hire. This would be an independent contractor and is limited to certain types of works, such as translations or where the piece is for a larger work.

Figure 8: U.S. Copyright Office Web site

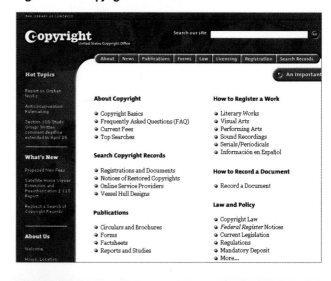

Adding a copyright notice

The familiar © symbol or "Copyright" is no longer required to indicate copyright, nor does it automatically register your work, but it does serve a useful purpose. When you post or publish it, you are stating clearly to those who might not know anything about copyright law that this work is claimed by you.

In a work for hire agreement, the copyright advantage is to the employer, plain and simple. Make sure you understand your arrangement very clearly. You can always negotiate a work for hire agreement to allow the creator some rights, such as being able to show the work in your portfolio.

Your legal case is made even stronger if someone violates your copyright and your notice is clearly visible.

The format of a copyright notice is as follows:

- Copyright symbol or word
- The year of first publication of the work
- The name of the copyright holder

Thus, proper notification is as follows:

Copyright 2009 Course Technology

or

© 2009 Course Technology

Your strongest legal position is established when you officially register a work with the Copyright Office.

Figure 9: Visual work of art section of copyright registration form

2 a

NOTE

Under the law, the "author" of a "work made for hire" is generally the employer, not the employee (see instructions). For any part of this work that was "made for hire" check "Yes" in the space provided, give the employer (or other person for whom the work was prepared) as "Author" of that part, and leave the space for dates of birth and death blank.

NAME OF AUTHOR ▼

DATES OF BIRTH AND DEATH
Year Born ▼   Year Died ▼

Was this contribution to the work a "work made for hire"?
☐ Yes
☐ No

Author's Nationality or Domicile
Name of Country
OR { Citizen of _____
Domiciled in _____

Was This Author's Contribution to the Work
Anonymous?   ☐ Yes ☐ No
Pseudonymous?   ☐ Yes ☐ No

If the answer to either of these questions is "Yes," see detailed instructions.

Nature of Authorship Check appropriate box(es). **See instructions**
☐ 3-Dimensional sculpture   ☐ Map   ☐ Technical drawing
☐ 2-Dimensional artwork   ☐ Photograph   ☐ Text
☐ Reproduction of work of art ☐ Jewelry design ☐ Architectural work

b

Name of Author ▼

Dates of Birth and Death
Year Born ▼   Year Died ▼

Was this contribution to the work a "work made for hire"?
☐ Yes
☐ No

Author's Nationality or Domicile
Name of Country
OR { Citizen of _____
Domiciled in _____

Was This Author's Contribution to the Work
Anonymous?   ☐ Yes ☐ No
Pseudonymous?   ☐ Yes ☐ No

If the answer to either of these questions is "Yes," see detailed instructions.

Nature of Authorship Check appropriate box(es). **See instructions**
☐ 3-Dimensional sculpture   ☐ Map   ☐ Technical drawing
☐ 2-Dimensional artwork   ☐ Photograph   ☐ Text
☐ Reproduction of work of art ☐ Jewelry design ☐ Architectural work

The specifics of searching for copyright

It is important to research whether a work you want to use already has copyright protection. You can search U.S. Copyright Office records in three databases: books, music, and other registered works; serials; and documents. The Copyright Office will search its records for you at $150 per hour to determine whether a work is still protected by copyright. Note that the Copyright Office cannot determine questions of possible infringement or determine the degree of similarity between multiple versions of a work. Remember that because copyright does not protect names and titles, records may list many different works identified by the same or similar titles. To further complicate matters, the title may have trademark protection. You can search trademarks and patents at the U.S. Patent and Trademark Office (www.uspto.gov).

What work is not copyright-protected?

Not all works are protected by copyright. Works that do not have or have lost copyright protection are said to be in the **public domain**. Regardless of a work's previous copyright status or how it comes to be in the public domain, the rules for its use are standard: You can modify, copy, and distribute public domain works as you please, for any purpose.

■ Many kinds of works, by their nature, are not protected by copyright:

- Ideas, facts, titles, slogans, discoveries, improvisational works, to name a few

  As you have seen, ideas and facts are not protected by copyright, although they might be protected by trademark or another category of intellectual property.

- The merger doctrine, when there are only a few ways to describe something

The **merger doctrine** applies when there is a *very* limited number of ways to express an idea. If someone could copyright that expression, they would have a monopoly on the idea, which copyright law does not allow. Therefore, where an idea and its expression are so intertwined, the expression can't be copyrighted. For example, rules for a contest or lottery usually sound the same because there are only a few ways to explain the legalities involved. In court cases involving computer software, defendants have invoked the merger doctrine because there are usually only a few *efficient* ways to write code that produces the desired result.

- Works that are stock scenes or elements, known as *scenes à faire.*

Figure 10: Examples of *scenes à faire*

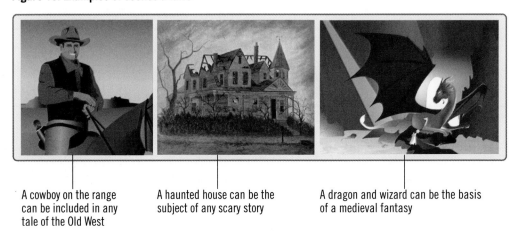

A cowboy on the range can be included in any tale of the Old West

A haunted house can be the subject of any scary story

A dragon and wizard can be the basis of a medieval fantasy

Using songs in work

The rights to a song can be jointly owned by the composer, lyricist, and the actual owner of the sound recording, which is usually a company. Copyright is enforced by organizations such as the American Society of Composers, Authors, and Publishers (ASCAP). Among the songs in ASCAP's collection is Woody Guthrie's "This Land Is Your Land," a perennial campfire chestnut. The song gained notoriety in the 2004 Presidential campaign after the Web animation site Jib Jab produced "This Land," a political parody. Ludlow Music, who thought they held the copyright to "This Land is Your Land," threatened to sue Jib Jab, contending that the work offered no "satirical comment" on the Guthrie original. It turned out Ludlow did not own rights to the song; it is in the public domain. If they had actually owned the rights, Jib Jab would have faced unpleasant legal action.

FYI

For a detailed look at when works enter the public domain, visit *www.unc.edu/~unclng/public-d.htm*.

Scenes à faire are stock scenes, characters, and features of a work considered standard or essential to the genre or field, as shown in **Figure 10**. For example, setting a tire commercial in a car driving down a rainy lonely road at night, starting a crime story with a mysterious beautiful woman walking into a private investigator's shabby office, or computer programs that use similar icons for performing functions such as opening, saving, and deleting files, are all examples of *scenes à faire*. A variety of cases involving software, music, and literary works have considered *scenes à faire* when determining infringement.

- Laws from all levels of government, including court decisions and legislation
- Federal government documents such as agency reports and Congressional hearings
- A phrase, title, slogan, or name (although these might be eligible for trademark protection)

■ Works can also enter the public domain for other reasons, such as the following:

- The copyright term expired.
- The owner did not renew the copyright.
- The owner did not properly obtain copyright protection (because the owner didn't follow the directions).
- The owner intentionally relinquished copyright protection for the work and placed it in the public domain.

You can modify, copy, and distribute public domain works as you please, for any purpose.

Many artists and software developers support and appreciate the significance of the public domain. These copyright holders value the public domain as a resource; they do not see the public domain as something into which works "fall, as if it were a dark abyss devoid of value."

■ How can I be sure a work is in the public domain?

Unfortunately, the date a work enters the public domain is not always obvious. It varies based on whether the work was published, whether it had a copyright notice, whether the copyright had been renewed, and combinations of those factors and more. You cannot always or easily determine whether a work still has copyright protection. Generally, works created and first published before January 1, 1923, or at least 95 years before January 1st of the current year, whichever is later, are in the public domain—but this is not always the case. The easiest way is to use work that clearly states or includes evidence that it is in the public domain.

Tattoos and copyright

The U.S. Copyright Office issued its first certificate of copyright for a tattoo in early 2006. Although on the surface tattoos might seem like a straightforward expression of an idea easily embraced by copyright law, in reality tattoos have had a distinctive relationship with the legal system and among tattoo artists. Traditionally, some tattoo artists have been leery of the legal system and have not undertaken suing for copyright infringement as a remedy. Likewise, the entertainment industry and other companies have not pursued copyright infringement against artists who routinely ink popular culture icons and even company logos.

Figure 11 shows a tattoo of the public domain Greek tragedy and comedy masks. Note that even if a tattoo image does not have copyright protection, a photograph of the image does. Modifying and even copying designs is an accepted practice, although with the explosion of unique one-of-a-kind images and inking styles, some artists have sought to assert their intellectual property rights. Artists can copyright or even trademark their work and negotiate a work for hire arrangement with clients so they maintain use of the design. They have pursued legal action against those who improperly use photographs of tattoos.

Figure 11: Copyright protection for a tattoo

How do I find media I can use?

Using a search engine to find public domain and open access work can prove time-consuming and oft-times ineffective. Fortunately, many Web sites can help narrow your search, by hosting or providing links to files of all media types you can use.

■ What sites contain public domain and open access media?

When performing your own media searches, the easiest places to look are photography, sound, and video sites; U.S. and state government agencies; the Library of Congress; universities; libraries; and organizational, personal, and commercial photo-sharing sites. Libraries in particular can be a great resource. Aside from having a wealth of material available online, their catalogs might also contain usable media not yet digitized or posted on their Web site. Some Web sites and blogs focus specifically on links to usable material. **Figure 12** shows the Internet Archive Web page, which houses thousands of public domain movies and films.

Another resource is the *Surf and Turf Index of Online Resources (STIOR)*, a table of public domain, open access, and sites of interest links for still images, clip art, video, animation, and sound, developed in conjunction with the Online Companion for this book: *Copyright on the Internet: Illustrated Essentials*. See **Figure 13**.

The concept of retaining certain rights to your work while promoting its general use is essential to progress and innovation.

Universities and public libraries hold unique collections that have been digitized and placed on their Web sites. Many of the images are in the public domain or have a relatively low fee associated with using them. Leading public libraries, such as the New York Public Library, have already digitized hundreds of thousands of photos and images of their vast holdings. In addition, photomuse.org, a collaboration of the George Eastman House and the International Center of Photography in Midtown Manhattan, is digitizing 200,000 masterwork photographs in searchable databases. Beyond government and commercial sources lies what could become the bedrock of file access: sites hosted by individuals who foster sharing media. These sites can contain media created solely by the host, collections of material compiled by the host, or files posted by hundreds of individuals who want to share their work.

Figure 12: The Internet Archive Web site

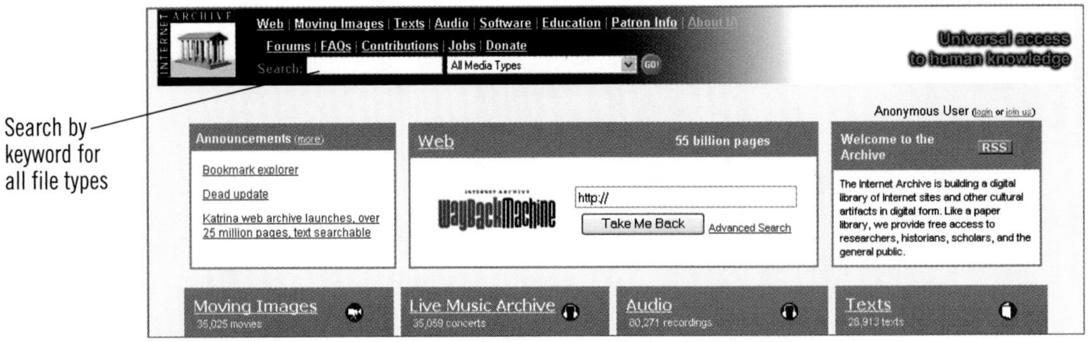

Search by keyword for all file types

Using Microsoft clip art

Owners of licensed Microsoft Office software can use clip art for personal or educational use, or for commercial use providing the clip art is not used in a logo and you do not resell the clip art in a collection. However, Microsoft cautions that the burden is on you to ascertain proper, noncommercial use. From the company's perspective, your compliance is presumed when you clicked the End License User Agreement (EULA) check box that appears during the software-loading process. However, the courts' enforceability of the license, also known as a quick wrap license, is not guaranteed.

A UNIT

What resources can help me find open access media?

The concept of retaining certain rights to one's work while promoting its general use is essential to progress and innovation; however, it can be difficult for individuals to so dedicate their work when copyright protection is automatic. This quandary is addressed by organizations such as Creative Commons, shown in **Figure 14**. Creative Commons is dedicated to building "a layer of reasonable, flexible copyright in the face of increasingly restrictive default rules." This organization makes registering and finding open access works much simpler. **Open access** is a type of licensing that allows a copyright holder to retain certain rights to their work while generously releasing the work for others to use.

Copyright owners can register works using the Creative Commons Web site. You can choose one of several types of license, ranging from requiring simple attribution for your work, to allowing sampling, to specifying no commercial use or no derivative use. Note that after you designate a work in the public domain or with an open access license, you cannot take it back or change it.

What sites contain public domain and open access media?

Creative Commons provides a search engine that retrieves results of open access or public domain works, and also includes an option to search just for works you can use commercially.

Before downloading anything, always locate the terms of use and make sure you understand them, especially if you are seeking content for commercial use.

What rights are "Reserved"?

There will be times when you find the perfect photo for a project on a site that states "All Rights Reserved." When a copyright holder uses that phrase, they are not necessarily saying "Go away, this work is off limits." But they are stating unequivocally that you must ask and receive permission before using the material. Chances are also that they would vigorously pursue any copyright infringement. The terms "All Rights Reserved" and "Some Rights Reserved" pertain to an international treaty; the language is no longer necessary, nor does it infer different protections. You can think of a Creative Commons license as "Some Rights Reserved."

Figure 13: Copyright on the Internet Online Resources Web site

Select media type for list of links

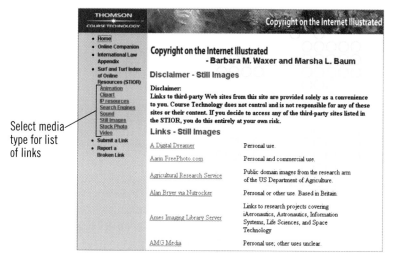

Figure 14: Creative Commons Web site

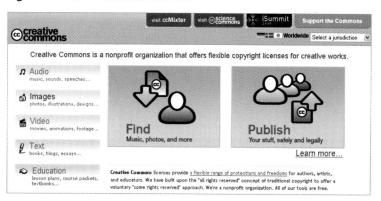

Imitation is said to be the highest form of flattery. But when that imitation or interpretation infringes on the rights of another artist, things can get complicated. As a creative artist, you must make sure that your use of influences and inspiration is proper.

Licensing—Musicians and Royalties

Royalty payments are a vital source of income for countless artists and other copyright owners. A **royalty** is a fee paid to a copyright owner for the right to use their work. Historically, many artists have been illegally denied copyright protection for their work and have suffered financially as a result. In the 1950s and 1960s, record companies, music publishers, and early rock and roll musicians, including Elvis Presley, The Beatles, The Rolling Stones, and Cream, made hits recording songs written by African-American musicians, and essentially stole royalties from the rightful songwriters. Years later, successful copyright infringement suits allowed musicians such as singer Ruth Brown to recoup royalties from Atlantic Records and songwriter and bassist Willie Dixon to settle out of court with Led Zeppelin. Led Zeppelin had taken Dixon's song "You Need Love" and changed it to "Whole Lotta Love" (which has sold millions of copies since 1969). Some nonprofit organizations such as the Blues Foundation (*www.blues.org*), shown in **Figure 15**, promote, preserve, and highlight Blues music education and history. Some have provided financial assistance to musicians, many of whom were denied royalties and copyright protections during their careers.

What About Fan Fiction?

Fan fiction consists of stories written by enthusiastic followers and devotees of a film, television show, or other work of fiction using the characters, setting, storylines, and so on of the original. It is an enormous field; there are tens of thousands of *Star Trek* and *Harry Potter* stories alone. Fan fiction obviously constitutes infringement and may be legally actionable unless the author grants permission for the use. With its range of topics (and ratings), fan fiction has a multitude of subgenres. Copyright owners, whether the creator, such as J.K. Rowling (*Harry Potter*) or a company, such as Paramount Pictures (*Star Trek*), may tolerate or even encourage fan fiction, as both Ms. Rowling and Paramount do. Others, such as Anne Rice (*Interview with the Vampire*) expressly forbid fan fiction and enforce their copyright protections to the fullest. The argument for fan fiction is that it takes nothing from and freely promotes the original, and is not written for profit. The argument against it is that it dilutes the value of the copyright.

> Early rock and roll musicians, including Elvis Presley, The Beatles, The Rolling Stones, and Cream, made hits recording songs written by African-American musicians, and essentially stole royalties from the rightful songwriters.

Regardless of the fact that some copyright owners permit fan fiction, writing a story using your favorite characters from a movie, book, or television show infringes the owner's copyright. You can write about ideas and plot overviews, but not characters that are "well-developed and sufficiently delineated." Determining if characters fit that description is decided on a case-by-case basis and differentiated between cartoon characters and literary characters. Cartoon characters that have "physical as well as conceptual qualities" are readily protected by copyright (and probably by trademark as well),

Figure 15: The Blues Foundation Web page

The Blues Foundation preserves the history of Blues music

whereas literary characters will be protected if they are so fully developed that the character stands out from the idea or plot behind the character. For example, Darth Vader, Luke Skywalker, and their neighborhood star system are not merely an emperor's enforcer who dresses in black, a young protector dressed in a white sashed shirt, and a galaxy far, far away.

Can Copyright Protect Different Things Having the Same Name?

Remember that you cannot copyright short phrases, terms, and titles, although there are exceptions. For example, a seller of coffee mugs was prohibited from using the phrase "ET phone home" on mugs because of copyright infringement because the phrase evoked the copyrighted character from the Universal Studios film *ET The Extraterrestrial*.

But, what about different works that have the same name? This is where performing a search at the Copyright Office becomes invaluable. Suppose, for example, you want to register a unique snowboard-related work for copyright protection. When you perform a search on "snowboard" at the Copyright Office, you find that many

skateboard-related items have copyright protection, shown in **Figure 16**, and include:

- Art design (clothing and watch)
- Book
- Screenplay
- Silk screen
- Jewelry
- Sculpture
- Needlework
- Stuffed animal
- Article and photographs from article in *National Geographic*

To register your work for copyright protection, you would need to determine not only that it is a unique expression, but that it would not be confused with nor take sales away from other products that use the word "snowboard."

Figure 16: Copyright-protected works using "snowboard"

Serials Database (Title Search)
Search For: SNOWBOARD

Check one or more terms, select the type of output display, and then click Submit:

☐ SNOW WEEK (1 item)
☐ SNOWBIRD MONTHLY (1 item)
☐ SNOWBOARD BUYER'S GUIDE (1 item)
☐ SNOWBOARD MAGAZINE (8 items)
☐ SNOWBOARD RESORT GUIDE (1 item)
☐ SNOWBOARDER (16 items)
☐ SNOWBOARDER MAGAZINE (16 items)
☐ SNOWBOUND (5 items)
☐ SNOWBREAK 1989 EDDIE BAUER CATALOG
☐ SNOWGOER (1 item)
☐ SNOWMASS AFFAIRS (10 items)
☐ SNOWMASS MAGAZINE (4 items)

Registered Works Database (Title Search)
Search For: SNOWBOARD

Check one or more terms, select the type of output display, and then click Submit:

☐ SNOWBLOWING WOODLAND SANTA WATERGLOBE (1 item)
☐ SNOWBO BOUQUET (1 item)
☐ SNOWBOARD (12 items)
☐ SNOWBOARD ACADEMY (2 items)
☐ SNOWBOARD ANGEL : NO. SBA-22 (1 item)
☐ SNOWBOARD BASICS (1 item)
☐ SNOWBOARD BEAR (5 items)
☐ SNOWBOARD BEAR BOY (1 item)
☐ SNOWBOARD BEAR GIRL (1 item)
☐ SNOWBOARD BEAR HORIZONTAL (1 item)
☐ SNOWBOARD BEAR, BOY (1 item)
☐ SNOWBOARD BEAR, GIRL (1 item)

Documents Database (Title Search)
Search For: SNOWBOARD

Check one or more terms, select the type of output display, and then click Submit:

☐ SNOWBLINDER (2 items)
☐ SNOWBLOSSOMS (8 items)
☐ SNOWBOARD (2 items)
☐ SNOWBOARD ACADEMY (12 items)
☐ SNOWBOARD BABES (2 items)
☐ SNOWBOARD BASICS (4 items)
☐ SNOWBOARD LEAVE ONLY TRACKS (6 items)
☐ SNOWBOARD SHARKS (4 items)
☐ SNOWBOARDER (2 items)
☐ SNOWBOARDER MAGAZINE SBTV: NO. 502, SICK DA (2 items)
☐ SNOWBOARDER MAGAZINE: NO. 501 (2 items)
☐ SNOWBOARDER MAGAZINE: NO. 503, FIELD REPORT (2 items)
Submit

Terms of Use

The rules that a copyright owner uses to establish use of their work are known as **terms of use**. Legally, there are two assumptions made whenever you download files, including software: 1) The material is protected by copyright; and 2) you have tacitly agreed to the terms posted on the site. This is true even if you never read the terms or didn't understand them. Ideally, the terms should clearly identify what can and cannot be done to the work on the site. **Figure 17** shows a few sample terms of use. When looking for copyright information on a Web site, you soon learn that there is no universal standard on where terms of use appear or how informative they are. Some copyright holders define their terms explicitly; others might use terms incorrectly or make their own assumptions, such as what constitutes personal or educational use.

Even when terms of use are clearly stated on a site, some users interpret them very loosely, or not at all. For example, many people genuinely believe that any file on the Internet on which you can right-click and save to disk is in the public domain—after all, it wouldn't be so easy to download if it weren't, right? Conversely, some Web sites erroneously assert copyright protection over public domain materials simply because they have placed them in their collection.

Even when you have the best intentions, you might find that your interpretation of a work's terms of use doesn't always match the copyright holder's. That is often because the terms include common words such as personal, educational, commercial, internal, corporate, nonprofit, free, and public domain, and those words mean different things to different people. For instance, most people assume "personal use" refers to one's private, not professional life. But one person might interpret it as sharing the work with a very limited audience of

Figure 17: Sample terms of use

DISCLAIMER: All of the sounds on our site are "Free for Non-Commercial Use" and you can download any sound that is on this site for FREE provided that you intend to use the sounds in a Non-Commercial Manner.

So the photos, graphics, designs or text I've produced and integrated into this website are not copyrighted. They are explicitly placed in the public domain. Use them for whatever you want. Use it all. Sell it. Mangle it. Whatever you want. Please. But it would be polite to let me know so I can at least enjoy whatever creative use you're putting it to.

The images MAY be used freely for personal, educational* and non-profit projects.

You may NOT use them commercially, claim authorship and/or sell them.

You must NOT redistribute the unaltered images and files in any way designed for reuse**.

* By educational use we are referring to assigned homework and school related projects.
** You may not include this images modified or unmodified on a diskette, CD, website or any other medium and offer them for redistribution or resale of any kind.

Most of the images on our Web pages are in the "public domain" (which means they have no copyright restrictions). If an image on our Web site is not restricted and does not say it is copyrighted, then you can assume it is in the public domain. You may download and use those copyright-free images in your print and electronic publications. There's no fee to pay (i.e., they're free), and no need to get permission from the Service for reusing them. As indicated in our Copyright Statement, permission is not needed to link to the Service's Web pages either.

friends and family. Another person might consider personal use to include a personal Web page (theoretically published for all to see), business or greeting card, or an avatar in a chat room or blog (an avatar is a graphical image of a person, such as a photograph or animated GIF, that represents the person speaking or playing). To some people, the definition of "educational use" might mean use by students and teachers in elementary and high school classes only, whereas to others it might indicate the instructor can use a work but students cannot. Similarly, people might not understand the full meaning of a term such as "for nonprofit use only." Many people assume that nonprofit groups are very small or volunteer-run organizations, but a nonprofit organization can range from a local cancer support group to a hospital with a staff of 7000 to an international disaster relief organization.

Locating Terms of Use

When searching for terms of use in a Web site, look for links such as Terms, Terms of Use, Copyright, FAQ, About Me, About Us, Use, Usage, Contact Us, and similar keywords. Sometimes you need to open the photos or image page before reaching the copyright links.

When looking for copyright information on a Web site, you soon learn that there is no universal standard on where terms of use appear or how informative they are.

Some sites post their terms of use prominently on the home page. Other sites state a specific use and then go on to explain that the material cannot be used, altered, copied, distributed, linked to, or transmitted without written permission. Note that many copyright holders who allow use of their material might also request that you notify them how you will be using the file, or they might, at the very least, request that you credit their work in some manner.

Photographing art in museums

Photographing any privately held work of art without permission infringes the copyright owner's rights. Even if the art is on public display, such as at a gallery or museum, the artist's copyright is still protected. If the work on display is in the public domain, you are legally within your rights to photograph it. But, after you enter the museum or gallery, such as the National Museum of the American Indian, shown in **Figure 18**, you are also bound by the rules of the facility. So, just as they can prohibit smoking, food, or beverages, they can also prohibit photography.

Figure 18: Museums can set their own terms of use for photographs

End of Unit Exercises

Key Terms

Author	Intellectual property	Public domain	Tangible medium of expression
Copyright	Intellectual property law	Right of privacy	Terms of use
Design patent	Merger doctrine	Right of publicity	Trade dress law
First sale doctrine	Open access	Ripping	Trade secret law
Idea-Expression Dichotomy	Original	Royalty	Trademark law
Intangible asset	Patent law	Scenes à faire	Work of authorship

Unit Review

1. Discuss why media files you can download from the Internet are not necessarily available to use as you want.

2. Explain how intellectual property differs from real or personal property, and what types of work it can include.

3. Describe three forms of a work of authorship.

4. List three tangible media of expression.

5. Think of and describe an original work of authorship and three potential derivative works.

6. Discuss how eliminating an author's right to create derivative works could affect his or her revenue.

7. Discuss the advantages of registering your work with the Copyright Office and including a copyright notification.

8. Discuss what is necessary for a work to be eligible for copyright protection and then describe why professional quality is or is not a factor.

9. Discuss the two purposes of copyright and an issue of concern associated with each.

10. For each of the following situations, identify whether you own the copyright and why: 1) a song you ripped from a CD you purchased; 2) a popular song you ripped from a friend's MP3 player; 3) a song you wrote yourself; and 4) a song you legally purchased and downloaded from the Internet.

Fill in the Best Answer

1. Copyright law is said to protect the expression of an idea but not the underlying ideas or facts themselves, in a rule of law known as the _____.

2. The number of fat grams in a cheeseburger, the countries that border Afghanistan, and requiring voters to show photo ID cannot be protected by copyright because they are examples of _____.

3. A romance about how opposites attract is an example of _____.

4. You can search for work that has the same name you want to use in a work at the _____.

5. In a work for hire agreement between a hired writer and a hiring employer, the copyright advantage is skewed to the _____.

6. The copyright notice, "Copyright Warner Brothers Studios" is missing the _____.

7. A limited number of ways of expressing an idea is not eligible for copyright protection and is known as the _____.

8. The payment to an author to use their work is known as a _____ payment.

9. Making a movie out of a book is a right of the author and an example of a _____ work.

10. Balancing public progress and an individual's right to benefit from their work is the purpose of _____ law.

Select the Best Answer

1. Which of the following is NOT an example of a derivative work made from a short film?

   a. A radio show based on the film's plot and characters

   b. A review of the film that includes quotes and stills

   c. A translation of the dialog in the film

   d. A screen saver using scenes from the film

2. You want to write a story about the history of text messaging for class. At what point is it protected by copyright?

   a. When you first think about it

   b. When you write it down

   c. When you register it with the Copyright Office

   d. When you present it in class

3. One important aspect of copyright law is that you own and control how your creation is used:

   a. Unless someone else wants to use it.

   b. Unless you dedicate the work to the public domain.

   c. After you register it with the Copyright Office.

   d. Unless your work is on the Internet.

4. If a work is in the public domain:

   a. You can create a derivative work from it only if no one does so first.

   b. You can use it however you want.

   c. You can only use it once.

   d. It must be very old.

5. The strongest legal position for protecting your copyright comes from:

   a. Registering it with the Copyright Office.

   b. Never posting it on the Internet.

   c. Including your name as part of the title of the work.

   d. Being the only source where someone can buy it.

6. Seeing the phrase "All Rights Reserved" on a Web site tells you:

   a. You will never be able to get permission to use the work.

   b. You may be able to get permission to use the work.

   c. You can reproduce the work as long as you don't alter it.

   d. You should check to make sure there isn't also a © symbol, and if there isn't one, use it.

7. Seeing the phrase "for educational use only" on two different Web sites tells you:

   a. You can use material from both sites if you're an instructor.

   b. You can use material from both sites if you're a student.

   c. You should find out what each Web site means by "educational use."

   d. You can use material from both sites as long as someone learns something.

8. An open access license means:

   a. The author retains some rights but promotes use of the work.

   b. The author has donated the work to the public domain.

   c. The author must give permission before you can use the work.

   d. The author doesn't care how you use the work.

9. Which of the following is the least likely source of public domain work?

   a. The online collection at the Chicago Public Library

   b. The Chicago Independent Film Festival

   c. The Antiquities collection at the Art Institute of Chicago

   d. The online collection at the Chicago Sun-Times of photographs created before 1919

10. Which of the following is NOT a myth associated with using images and media on the Internet?

    a. If you can download it, you can use it.

    b. You can always get permission later if you get caught.

    c. Most people will thank you for downloading their work.

    d. Your agreement to a site's terms of use is implicit.

End of Unit Exercises

INDEPENDENT CHALLENGE 1

You've had an idea for an animated character in your head and have talked about it with your friends for years. One day, you sketch out the character using pen and paper and name it *Tex TipTop*. You give a copy of the sketch to a friend who does 3D animation, and you ask her to help you to fill in details and smooth it out. She does all that and more. Unbeknownst to you, she creates an entire storyline around your character and makes it into a 3D animated film that wins the top prize at an online film festival. In the credits, she thanks you "for your idea."

Based on your knowledge of copyright, answer the following questions.

1. Who owns the copyright to Tex TipTop's name, the overall character, and his specific attributes? Include arguments for and against both sides, and then state which you believe is correct.

2. Based on your answer, who can make Tex TipTop into an action figure and why?

3. Who do you think owns the movie, and why?

INDEPENDENT CHALLENGE 2

You find a great photo on the Web, download it to your computer, modify the photo with one of your own photos in an image-editing program such as Adobe Photoshop, and then silk-screen it onto 20 shirts.

1. Based on your knowledge of copyright, identify whether the following are copyright myths or facts, and give the reason for your answer.

   a. There was no copyright symbol on the Web page where you found the photo, so it is not protected by copyright.

   b. Because the photo was freely available on the Web, it is in the public domain.

   c. The picture looked really old, so it is probably in the public domain.

2. Based on your answers, read the following statements and identify any rights of the original author that might have been violated.

   a. You're going to donate the shirts for a charity's silent auction so you won't make any money off of it.

   b. You're not selling the photo, just the shirt.

   c. You plan to send half of the proceeds from your t-shirt sales to the Web site where you found the photo.

INDEPENDENT CHALLENGE 3

Having a basic working knowledge of how work for hire agreements operate can prove essential to retaining or obtaining the copyright for a work. Because legal language is usually daunting and definitely not user-friendly, it's always a good idea to have an attorney read over any contract. Assess the following scenarios and determine who owns the copyright to the work described. Support your answers with examples from the text.

1. Jayden is a graphic designer at Solar System Advertising. He created a logo and product brand for a client's new line of luggage. Everything about the advertising campaign is a huge hit and people are even using the logo as their instant messaging avatar.

2. Although she works as a software developer, Sukiko is known to be a great artist. The company president, Ms. Ivana Berich, runs into Sukiko at the vending machine and asks her to design an art piece of her choice for the foyer in Ms. Berich's home.

3. Paul has a graphics business and is hired to add an animated bird to a scene in a television sitcom. The scene is already shot, so he must create a bird that matches the scene. The producers told him that they'd like the bird to be blue, but the rest of the bird's appearance is up to him.

INDEPENDENT CHALLENGE 4

You spend way too much time at a coffee house. The owner posts the daily special on a large board next to the counter and you've been recording how long customers spend reading the special and then correlate that amount of time to the number of customers who actually order it. You divide your findings by time of day and gender, and compile the results in Excel. In the hopes of getting free food and coffee, you name your new "business" Morebucks Investigatives, sell the results to the owner, and give him a copy of the Excel file as well as a printout. Next week, you notice a four-color graph of the results posted on the specials board.

Has the coffee shop used your work improperly? Discuss why or why not by addressing the following points:

1. Did your work meet the conditions necessary for a work to be eligible to be protected by copyright? Why or why not?

2. Did your work fit one of the types of work that can be copyright protected? Why or why not?

A Web site's terms of use govern your use of its media. Take the time to read and follow them, and you might find you have access to more media than you thought.

1. Review the terms of use shown in Figure 19.

Figure 19

Copyright Notice:
The content presented within this web site is copyrighted exclusivley to the creators of FreeMediaGoo.com. This content is available for both commercial and private use free of charge. All content contained within FreeMediaGoo.com may not be used for propaganda, pornographic or suggestive materials.

At the same time we allow Private Non Commercial Users to download images from our web site as long as you follow the simple rules outlined below.

So feel free to use any of the images on the site if you are a private individual and your use is not commercial.

All we ask is that you follow these simple rules.

The pictures are only available free for your own PERSONAL, NONCOMMERCIAL use and TEST or SAMPLE use, including COMPS and LAYOUTS.

You must credit the FreeFoto.com web site on your home page.

If you use one of the full screen images you must place a hypertext link with the line Supplied by FreeFoto.com in a conspicuous place.

You MAY NOT use the images to create your own photo gallery web site. If you want to use a picture on your own web page YOU MUST save the picture to your own hard disk and place it on your own server..

We also ask that you add a (c) FreeFoto.com to the image alt tag.

About

This project aims to create an archive of clip art that can be used for free for any use.

All graphics submitted to the project should be placed into the Public Domain according to the statement by the Creative Commons. If you'd like to help out, please join the mailing list. Also, browse the archives to review the project's history.

2. Use your favorite search engine to find three sites that offer "free" work.

3. Copy and paste their terms of use in a document, and then note how easy or difficult it was to locate the terms, that is, how far into the Web page structure you needed to click before you found the information.

4. Compare the terms you found with those shown in Figure 19, and then answer the following questions:

- What was the name of the link that displayed the terms of use?
- Is the content clearly identified to be protected by copyright or public domain?
- What limitations does the copyright holder place on the work?
- What does the copyright owner ask in return for use?
- Does the site define terms such as "educational" or "personal"?
- What is the quality of the images or media?
- Would you use the media from the sites you found? Explain why or why not.

Unauthorized Use
and Fair Use

What is copyright infringement?
How do you prove copyright infringement?
What can happen if I infringe someone's work?
How do I obtain permission to use someone's work?
What is fair use?
How do I piece together the copyright puzzle?
Is unauthorized use really wrong?

Topics and Inquiries: Educational fair use and parody
Copyright in Context: Innovation versus protection

Overview

This unit examines copyright infringement (the unauthorized use of a copyright-protected work) and fair use (the provisions that allow use of a protected work without permission). How you feel about copyright infringement often depends on which role you play in the infringement scenario—the person who holds the copyright to a work, or the one who wants to use it. If the work is downloadable from the Internet, the variables are even more complex; tools such as file-sharing software make potential infringement even easier, so deciding whether and how you can use the work can be more difficult. To be an informed and empowered decision maker, you need to understand what constitutes infringement, how to seek permission to use a copyrighted work, and also how to apply the fair use doctrine.

What is copyright infringement?

The term copyright infringement means unauthorized use of someone's intellectual property. U.S. copyright law allows for exceptions to an author's copyright, known legally as **limitations**, but before you can understand the limitations, you need a clear sense of what constitutes infringement. The criteria and determinants of infringement vary depending on what type of intellectual property is in question, but the common denominator in all cases is that someone has used someone else's exclusive right to their intellectual property without permission.

■ **Copyright infringement** is the violation of one or more of the rights granted to a copyright owner by using work without permission or without paying a royalty payment. Infringement can take many forms, including:

- Making a copy of a work by downloading it to your hard drive
- Taking a photograph of a work and then using it in your work
- Distributing copyrighted music over the Internet
- Creating a new musical work by sampling an existing work
- Building a house from a copyrighted design
- Inline linking (displaying an image from a copyrighted Web site on your Web site)
- Showing a copyrighted movie in a public place (which constitutes a performance of the work)

■ How do you know if it's infringement?

The courts decide whether someone has infringed the copyright of a work. The legal test for infringement asks the question whether the work has been copied in some manner.

When deciding infringement cases, judges consider the extent of the use. Most importantly, the court looks at whether there is substantial similarity between the copyrightable elements, such as design elements, characters, plot, or musical motifs. **Substantial similarity** looks at the degree to which a copy resembles the original copyrighted work. It does not have to consist of exact copying (although it can), such as line-by-line or pixel-by-pixel, but asks the question whether an ordinary observer would recognize that the copy is based on the original work. This is why you cannot enlarge or reduce an original work, or alter it in a significant way or amount. You will learn in a later lesson that using even small amounts of work can also violate copyright. This standard is not always crystal clear in practice, and the courts decide each case individually. **Figure 20** lists different examples of copyright infringement from several famous cases.

■ What is the difference between theft, copyright infringement, and plagiarism?

Many of us think of theft as meaning any illegal appropriation of someone else's property. Thus, posting a copyrighted photograph

Figure 20: Examples of copyright infringement

ACTION	EXAMPLE	INFRINGEMENT?
Consciously or unconsciously copying music into your own work	George Harrison unconsciously copied motif from "He's So Fine" by The Chiffons in "My Sweet Lord"	Yes
Peer-to-peer file sharing	Napster, Grokster, BitTorrent	Yes
Sampling music 1. Sampling a few notes that results in minor or insignificant use 2. Sampling hundreds of songs (to decide which ones you might buy)	Beastie Boys vs. James Newton The people the RIAA pursues for illegal downloading	No Yes
Creating an item in the shape of a copyrighted or trademarked item	Ferdinand Pickett created a guitar in the shape of the symbol associated with the artist formerly known as Prince	Yes
Singing all or part of a copyrighted song in public or using it in a film or TV show	The song "Happy Birthday To You"	Yes
Showing a copyrighted work incidentally in a scene for a few seconds in a film or TV show	A quilt hanging on a wall was featured prominently in the background of a TV show for 27 seconds	Yes

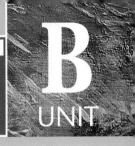

FYI

Copying that lacks significance or is so minor that it lacks grounds for infringement is known as *de minimis*.

of a Mustang on a Web site, stealing a Mustang GT from someone's driveway, and copying the song "Mustang Sally" can all be seen as examples of theft. In the legal landscape, stealing physical items is called theft and is punishable under criminal law; "stealing" or "pirating" copyrighted works is infringement of the rights of the copyright owner, and is punishable under civil law. **Plagiarism** occurs when you quote an amount of a *written* work and do not attribute the words to the author. The problem is not that you're quoting text, it's that you are not providing credit by attributing the work to the author. Although plagiarism is generally considered an academic offense (for which students can suffer consequences ranging from a failing grade to outright dismissal), it is not punishable under civil law; however, it can easily morph into infringement when you use extensive or substantial amounts of the work.

The common denominator in all cases [of infringement] is that someone has used someone else's exclusive right to their intellectual property without permission.

It is important to understand that attribution, although a great standard practice, is *never* a defense against infringement. In other words, giving credit to the copyright holder of a song or photo indicates that you are not trying to claim the work as your own, but it doesn't mean you are using the work properly, with permission. **Figure 21** compares the differences between plagiarism and copyright infringement.

Figure 21: Comparing plagiarism and copyright infringement

	PLAGIARISM	INFRINGEMENT
What's affected	Written work	Any work of authorship
Classification	Academic dishonesty	Copyright law violation
Effect	Fools reader into believing you wrote the work	Denies copyright owner reward for creation
Consequence	Failing grade; expulsion; loss of degree, job, or publishing contract	May be liable for damages; can no longer use material
How to avoid consequences	Give proper credit to author or source	Obtain permission from owner to use the work

Understanding legal lingo

In a legal setting, the words infringement and violation have special meaning. In intellectual property, you can *infringe* someone's copyright, patent, or trademark, whereas rights of publicity and privacy are said to be *violated*. And, if you are ever sued and the court finds that you have indeed infringed or violated, you are *liable*, not guilty. The legal system does not brand you as a pirate, thief, or bandit. It's most important that you understand the concepts behind the laws, regardless of the words you use.

How do you prove copyright infringement?

Some people infringe copyright because they don't realize they are breaking any laws. Others deliberately infringe, believing that the copyright holder will not mind, will not notice, or won't feel an economic impact from the infringement. Regardless of intent, after you venture into the legal landscape, you will find very specific procedures and requirements that must be met if pursuing or defending against a copyright infringement suit.

■ **What must be proven to make a case?**

Copyright infringement can be either direct or indirect. Direct infringement is when you violate one of a copyright owner's exclusive rights. To prove **direct infringement** in a civil copyright infringement case, the copyright owner must establish the following elements:

■ The work is protected by copyright (and registered with the Copyright Office).

■ The infringer has copied the work, as shown by the following:

   • The infringer's admission (rare, but it happens)

   • The copyright owner offering circumstantial evidence of infringement by demonstrating that the alleged infringer had *access* to the work and that the alleged infringing work was *substantially similar* to the copyrighted work

■ The use of the work was improper—the alleged infringer copied the protected expression. You have to prove that not only did the person copy your work (as opposed to copying someone else's work or creating it independently), but they also took your creative elements, the *protected expression*, from your copyrighted work. The test for improper use might be verbatim copying of the whole work (a reproduction), copying a part of the work (sampling), or copying the "total concept and feel" of your work. Examples include a character in a story, the user interface of a computer program, or the theme or design of an ad campaign that so closely resembles your creation that the ordinary observer would think they were similar.

Even if you are unaware of the infringing activity, you can still be liable for the infringement.

You can also be held liable through **indirect infringement**, in which you do not directly infringe a copyright, but you aid someone else's infringing conduct. There are two types of indirect infringement, contributory infringement and vicarious infringement, as shown in **Figure 22**. **Contributory infringement** is conduct that assists the infringement, such as providing a product whose use is

Figure 22: Direct versus indirect infringement

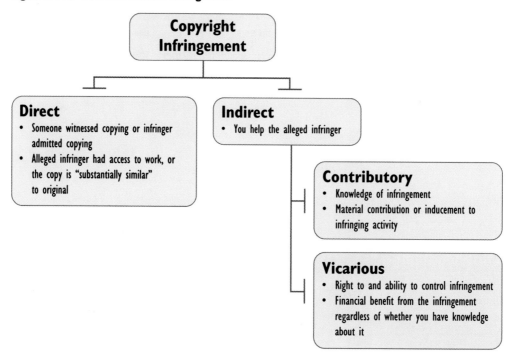

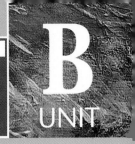
FYI

The statute of limitations on copyright infringement cases is three years.

central to another person's ability to infringe. You can think of contributory infringement as conduct that induces or encourages the infringing behavior. Examples include advertising to users that your file-sharing software can download any music and movie for free. Note that in trademark law, it occurs when someone distributes a product that is then "passed off" as something that is subject to trademark protection, such as selling an off-brand cola in a restaurant that has Coca-Cola signs posted.

Vicarious infringement occurs when you have the "right and ability to supervise the infringing activity" and a financial interest in supporting that infringement. In other words, you might know that infringement is going on and you benefit financially from the infringing action. Even if you are unaware of the infringing activity, you can still be liable for the infringement. For example, you are liable for vicarious infringement if you own a flea market and rent a booth to

someone who sells bootleg CDs and DVDs, even if you don't know they are selling such things. Vicarious infringement has particularly come into prominence with the development of digital copying and file-sharing technology. Suppose you create file-sharing software that searches individual computers but you have no way of knowing what the search query is or what users are downloading. Users can use the program to download legal or illegal content. The fact that they *can* download illegal files makes you liable. The courts now lean toward seeing developing technology that *could* be used to facilitate copyright infringement to be the same as actually infringing. **Figure 23** shows examples of contributory and vicarious infringement.

Finally, you should note that there is no "five-second" rule in copyright infringement. Keeping an illegally downloaded song on your computer for 12 hours does not make for any less infringement than if you kept it on your computer for 12 years.

Figure 23: Sample vicarious and contributory infringement scenarios

Vicarious infringement

Contributory infringement

Running a flea market and renting a booth to someone who sells bootleg copies of CDs and DVDs

Advertising and selling software on the Internet that can crack any program

Hosting a Web and chat site for popular movies and allowing members to upload and download protected images and snippets

Knowingly providing a link to sites that contain unlicensed songs and video

Understanding the legal setting for infringement suits

Copyright infringement cases are, for the most part, based on civil law, not criminal law. The distinction between the two is significant. The assumptions and burdens of proof governing copyright infringement are less rigorous in civil law than they would be in criminal law. In civil law, there is never the need to show infringement beyond a reasonable doubt, and there might even be an assumption of "guilt"—that is, responsibility. In a copyright infringement case, as soon as the copyright owner has met the burden of establishing a *prima facie* case (alleged evidence sufficient to prove a case), the burden

shifts onto the alleged infringer to prove that he or she did not infringe. For example, U.S. copyright law specifically prohibits removing a watermark from a photograph. You can be sued for removing a watermark, even if that's all you do, because the act itself is viewed by the court as evidence of your intent to violate the owner's copyright. The assumption is that you are liable and you must prove that you're not. It is a stark contrast to criminal law, where the defendant in a criminal matter is presumed innocent until proven guilty, and the burden is on the prosecution to prove guilt beyond a reasonable doubt.

What can happen if I infringe someone's work?

Plain and simple: if you use copyrighted material without permission, you are setting yourself up for potentially unpleasant and expensive legal action. As you learned in the previous lesson, you can be held liable for infringing copyright even if you were unaware you were doing it. Exactly what happens if you get caught depends on many factors.

■ What happens first?

If you are found using someone's copyrighted work without permission, such as posting protected content on a Web page or illegally downloading music or film, you will likely first receive a **cease and desist letter**, a formal request for you to stop the infringing action. A cease and desist letter serves as official notice that someone believes you have infringed their copyright, and it should be taken seriously. Such a letter states when and how you copied the work without permission, demands that you immediately stop the use and distribution of said work, and demands that you respond that you have performed this action by a certain date. Otherwise, further legal action can and will be taken against you. **Figure 24** shows a sample cease and desist letter.

> If you use copyrighted material without permission, you are setting yourself up for potentially unpleasant and expensive legal action.

Students who infringe copyright might first receive notification by their educational institutions. University policy might result in a warning and perhaps require they take a tutorial in copyright. If they infringe again, they can lose some or all access privileges to the university computer network, face more serious academic disciplinary action, and even civil action.

■ What should I do next?

Should you find yourself in a legal action, the best first step is to seek competent legal advice. Relying instead on advice from your friends, something you heard about, or soothing your bruised ego by protesting that you didn't know you did anything wrong might seem a cheaper alternative, but most defendants can't afford to do without the guidance of an attorney who specializes in intellectual property law. Of course, the most economical course is to avoid the lawsuit in the first place, although this is not always possible.

If you believe that you have not infringed, or that your use is permissible, you can reply to that effect and see what action the accuser takes next. The main defense to copyright infringement is to prove that your use was a fair use (you learn more about claiming fair use in the next lesson). If you believe that indeed you have infringed, you should remove the material immediately. You can always repost the content if the legal matter is settled in your favor.

■ What happens if I lose?

If your defense is unsuccessful and you are found liable for copyright infringement, remedies for the copyright owner can be quite stiff, including the following:

- Receiving an injunction to stop your publication or distribution or performance or display of the infringing work
- Having the infringing items (which can include your entire work) impounded and destroyed

Understanding trademark infringement penalties

In addition to copyright infringement, you need to be concerned with possible trademark infringement for various materials you might be interested in using. Slogans, phrases, designs, images, characters, and symbols can all be trademarked. If you infringe a trademark, the possible penalties include the following:

- Injunction against use of the mark or use only under certain conditions
- Destruction of infringing articles

Monetary damages can include the following:

- The entirety of your profits
- The trademark owner's damages
- Court costs
- Possibly attorney's fees

- Paying actual damages to the copyright owner, such as lost profits or statutory damages of (as of this writing) between $750 and $30,000, which can be increased to $150,000 for **willful infringement** or reduced to not less than $250 for innocent infringement

Statutory damages are only available if the work was registered with the Copyright Office. The infringement is considered willful if, for example, you infringe a work that has posted a copyright notice. The courts respond to willful infringement very strongly. Willful copyright infringement is a federal crime, punishable by fines or even imprisonment. Prosecution for criminal copyright infringement, however, is rare.

Innocent infringement is when you were not aware that the material was protected. It does not mean you are not liable for damages, just that the amount you pay would be less than if you did know the work was copyrighted and used it anyway, whether because you thought your use was fair or because you didn't care that the work was protected. Remember that ignorance of the law is not an excuse, so saying "But I thought I could use anything posted on the Internet" would not make a good claim for innocent infringement. In a very simplified analogy, suppose you are cited for driving with broken tail lights. You won't get out of the ticket by arguing that you didn't know it was illegal to drive without tail lights or that you couldn't see the lights were broken because you were driving the car.

- Paying court costs and attorney's fees (at the discretion of the court)

Figure 24: Sample cease and desist letter sent to infringer

March 16, 2009

Dear Jane U. Infringer,

It has come to our attention that you have posted various elements of original content from www.EyeMCool.com on your Web site, located at www.WeRCooler.com.

These elements are protected by copyright. Your unauthorized use of this original material violates the copyrights owned by EyeMCool.com.

Based on this action, we require that you confirm to us in writing within 10 days that: 1) You have removed all infringing materials from your site and 2) You will discontinue any future posting of protected material.

Your failure to respond will leave us no choice but to pursue legal action against you.

Yours truly,
Amanda B. Reckonwith, JD
Glazed, Hamms, and Moore
representing EyeMCool.com

How do I get permission to use someone's work?

Thousands of copyright holders of various media are committed to sharing their content outright. Many simply expect that you ask permission—which is exactly within their legal rights. Still others might require that you pay a fee, which might be surprisingly within your price range or well worth the value you are receiving. You can enrich your educational, professional, and personal projects with wonderful online content while minimizing the risk of a legal action being brought against you if you practice due diligence in searching for content and gathering permissions.

■ How do I obtain permission?

Your permissions request should include specifics about what you want to use (text, photographs, music, trademarks, merchandise, and so on) and how you want to use it (school paper, personal Web site, book illustration, art piece). Obviously, getting permission from an amateur photographer whose work you found on a photo-sharing Web site might be easier than getting permission from a large music publisher. How you want to use the work determines the level and scope of permissions you need to secure; getting permission to stage a school play differs from permission to cover a Top 40 song in your debut CD. The fundamentals, however, are the same. Your request should contain the following:

- Your full name, address, and complete contact information

- A specific description of your intended use; sometimes including a sketch, storyboard, or link to a Web site is helpful

- A signature line for the copyright holder

- A target date when you would like the copyright holder to respond; this can be important if you're working under a deadline

A sample request letter is shown in **Figure 25**.

How you want to use the work determines the level and scope of permissions you need to secure.

■ What is the base assumption for use?

Not surprisingly, your assumption should be that you do not have permission to use a work until you actually receive it. You absolutely cannot benefit by inserting language in your permission letter such as "If I do not hear back from you within one month I will assume you have given me permission to use the work." There is no time limit for a copyright owner to write you back. A copyright owner is under no obligation to even respond to a request; silence is their prerogative, it

Figure 25: Sample permissions request

[Your name & contact info]
[Date]
[Name and address of copyright holder]

Dear *[Copyright Holder]*

I am *[describe who you are]*. I would like permission to use *[name of work & location]* for *[purpose, including how, where, frequency, modification]*.

Please complete the information at the bottom of this page and return the original to me in the enclosed stamped enevelope. I have also enclosed a copy for your records.

If you are not the copyright holder of this material, please let me know.

Thank you for your time and assistance.

Sincerely,

[Your signature]

[Your printed name]

_____

I grant permission for the use of the above material

Signature _____ Date _____
Credit line: _____

does not equate with consent. Legally, you would harm your legal standing considerably if you were to use a work for which you had requested, but not received, permission. Your actions tell the court that you knew the work had copyright protection, which makes you a willful infringer.

■ What about multimedia?

The issue of getting permission becomes even more complicated when you consider using music or multimedia. Obtaining permission to use music requires that you obtain rights to the song itself (written sheet music) and the rights to the particular recording. Therefore, you might need to locate the lyricist, the composer, and the owner of the sound recording.

Multimedia and documentary film making present an even bigger challenge. By definition, multimedia can contain video, animation, text, still photos or graphics, and sound, and each work can have its own creator or creators. It is also important to realize that the creator might or might not be the sole copyright owner, or might not be the copyright owner at all. You have to obtain permission from each copyright holder in each medium, which can prove a bit tricky, as shown in **Figure 26**. Fortunately, many sources have a permissions link on their Web site.

Figure 26: Sources to contact to obtain permission for media

Media	Possible Contacts
Print and Web text	Writer, publisher, Web site owner; if image is of a celebrity, right of publicity protection may be involved
Music and audio	Composer, songwriter, lyricist, record label; if public performance, ASCAP or BMI licensing organizations
Film and video	Production company, distributor, actors, director, producer, screenwriter
Still images and art	Creator, museum, gallery; if printed image, publisher

Making sure you ask the right person

Depending on the work, the creator might not always be the copyright holder; they might have sold or granted their copyright to a publisher, a record company, a film studio, or another person or company. When requesting permissions, it is important that you locate the true copyright owner. For example, documentary filmmaker Jon Else shot a 4.5-second scene of San Francisco Opera stagehands in a backstage room watching television (which happened to be showing an episode of *The Simpsons*) during an opera performance. He had permission to use everything except the few seconds of the *Simpsons* episode. He obtained permission from *Simpsons* creator Matt Groening and the show's production company, Gracie Films. However, the Fox Broadcasting Company, Gracie's parent company, refused to grant permission for Else to use the work for free and charged him $10,000 for the few seconds of inadvertent screen time. Mr. Else elected to delete the *Simpsons* material and edit in other work instead.

What is fair use?

You can use a work however you want *if*: it is not copyrightable to begin with; it is in the public domain; you have permission; or your use meets the criteria for fair use. A decision on fair use is dependent on the specific facts of the situation—and there is no set formula that stipulates how much of a work you can use. Nevertheless, by understanding the basics of the fair use doctrine, you can reasonably assess whether you can make a strong fair use argument for using copyrighted material you find on the Internet.

■ What is the fair use doctrine?

The fair use doctrine formally became a part of the copyright statute in 1976. **Fair use** is the foremost limitation upon, or exception to, copyright protection. It permits the public to use copyrighted material for certain purposes without obtaining prior consent from the owner. But, there are no hard-and-fast rules on what is considered fair use. The doctrine is always applied on a case-by-case basis, which can make it a difficult concept to grasp.

The fair use doctrine identifies four factors that the courts weigh when considering whether a use is fair. **Figure 27** details the four factors and illustrates what would likely be considered fair use.

Factor 1: The purpose and character of the use

Factor 2: The nature of the copyrighted work

Factor 3: The amount and substantiality of the portion used in relation to the copyrighted work as a whole

Factor 4: The effect of the use on the market or the potential market for the copyrighted work

---

There is no set formula that stipulates how much of a work you can use.

■ Under **Factor 1**, how you intend to use the work guides whether you can. Examples include nonprofit educational, news reporting, scholarship, research, and transformative. Rather than simply repeating the original work, the work must be **transformative**, which refers to altering the work so that the user or reader receives some new meaning or message. Note that educational use does *not* automatically equate to fair use; even though the use might be educational, it might still violate copyright. You learn more specifically about educational fair use later in this unit.

Examples: People who have been featured in *The Daily Show* would probably not ever give permission if they knew they'd be parodied. But because these parodies are satirical—that is, they comment on or ridicule social, political, or moral principles—they are considered transformative. Or, as a film student, you might want to compare the directing styles of Alfred Hitchcock and Martin Scorsese; your use of their film clips is transformative because it sheds new light on their use of framing and camera angles.

■ **Factor 2** looks at whether the work is a factual or creative work. An expression of fact is said to have "thin" copyright unless the expression is extremely creative. The facts themselves cannot be copyrighted because they are like ideas—discoverable but not protectable by copyright.

Example: A database that maps the number of bald eagle nests in Great Lakes states is obviously factual and so has thinner copyright than an animated film featuring bald eagle characters living in Great Lakes states and talking about their habitats. Or, providing links in your Web site to other Web sites is not considered copyright infringement—a hyperlink is a fact: a URL address that points to its location on the Internet. It does become a bit complicated if the link is to a site whose content infringes on someone else's copyright.

FYI

You cannot use a fair use argument to force a copyright owner to turn over a work so you can use it.

- **Factor 3** looks at *either* the amount or portion of the work you intend to copy or use. Note that the courts do not care if you only used 12 percent of a work, or 17 images out of 100. The amount that you didn't use is not a defense, as the courts have consistently held that "you cannot escape liability by showing how much of [a] work you did not take." Also, depending on the work, courts value the qualitative "heart of the work" over the amount you take from the whole. The amount you take might be small, but if it is key or central to the work, you cannot use it. Generally, the more you use, either proportionately or in its value to the overall work, the stronger the argument against fair use.

Example: If, when making your own film, showing a few seconds of an incidental scene from a science fiction movie is fair use, compared to showing a key scene where the alien is revealed or killed, or printing the most memorable part of a novel or song lyric.

- **Factor 4** examines the market for the copyrighted work. The courts have tended to focus on this factor by assessing the impact of the work on the market of the copyrighted work, often weighting it most of the four factors. If your work has any effect on the market for the copyrighted work, which can be beneficial or adverse, this factor weighs against fair use. Also included in the assessment are potential markets for the original work and its derivatives.

Example: Copying a protected work into a different medium, such as making a sculpture from a copyright-protected photograph of kids eating ice cream or posting a computer game on your Web site that would have adverse effects on the market for the original work you copied.

Figure 27: Analyzing the four factors of fair use

Factor	Fair Use	Unlikely Fair Use
Factor 1 Purpose and character of use	• Nonprofit educational purpose • Different purpose – transformative use – Commentary – Criticism – News reporting – Parody • Research • Scholarship	• Commercial – profit • Same purpose as original work – use not transformative • Entertainment (not parody)
Factor 2 Nature of copyrighted work	• Work is fact or nonfiction • Published work • Informational	• Original work has strong copyright (creative) • Unpublished work (copyright owner gets to decide if work will be made public)
Factor 3 Amount (quantity and quality)	• Small amount (relative to whole) • Portion used is not key to work	• Large amount • Heart of the work – central to work
Factor 4 Effect on the market	• No effect on the market of the original work (either positively or negatively)	• Major effect on existing or potential market • Replaces sales of original – appeals to same market • License or royalty payment was reasonable and could have been paid • Work is made available to entire world

How do I piece together the copyright puzzle?

You have learned that you should always presume that a work is protected by copyright and that if you want to use it you must determine its copyright status and then take appropriate steps from there. From that safe (if potentially daunting) first assumption, you can follow a simple method for ascertaining exactly what, if any, limits to using the material exist, and decide whether your intended use of the work would infringe the owner's copyright. This lesson provides guidance for determining whether you can use a work, and examines some relevant copyright infringement cases.

■ How do I determine if I can use the work?

Understanding the public domain, open access licensing, how to obtain permission for copyright-protected works, and fair use can be quite a challenge. To help make decisions when you want to use a specific work, refer to the diagram shown in **Figure 28**. This flowchart helps you negotiate the various paths from copyright protection to use. It offers a simple series of steps to help you determine whether you can use a file.

Figure 28: Decision chart for determining if you can use a work

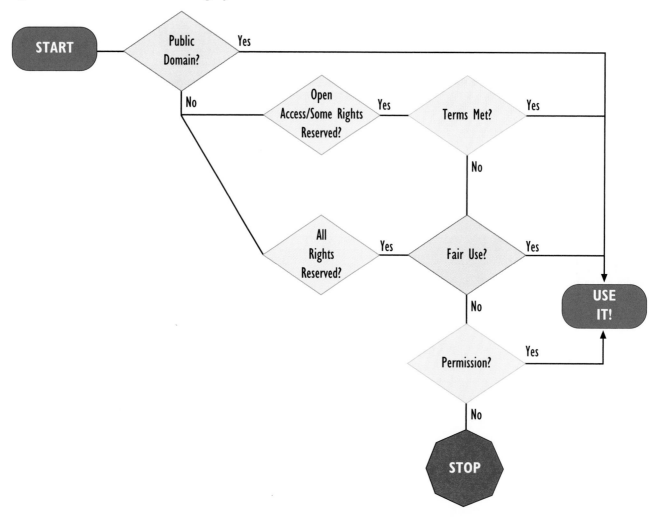

FYI

You should perform a fair use analysis each time you consider using a protected work.

■ What can I learn from examples of fair use?

The courts consider four factors—Purpose, Nature, Amount, and Effect—when determining fair use. To guide you when making fair use decisions, it might be helpful to see how the courts have weighed these four factors in actual infringement cases. **Figure 29** shows case facts, the prevailing arguments for each of the four factors, and the court rulings. As you can see, the decision on whether infringement has occurred is based on an on-balance assessment of all four factors.

Understanding the public domain, open access licensing, how to obtain permission for copyright-protected works, and fair use can be quite a challenge.

Figure 29: Following court rulings through the four factors of fair use

The Facts	Factor 1 Purpose	Factor 2 Nature	Factor 3 Amount	Factor 4 Effect	Ruling
Copy shop made and sold coursepacks that included excerpts and chapters from copyrighted works	Shop claimed educational use, courts found it was for commercial use (weighs against fair use)	Works were predominately factual — history & sociology (weighs for fair use)	5–25% from each book (no permission or payment for use) (weighs against fair use)	Coursepacks directly competed with book sales (weighs against fair use)	NOT FAIR USE
Author published a trivia book based on the TV show *Seinfeld*	Trivia are not transformative; commercial use (weighs against fair use)	The source material, Seinfeld, is a television show — creative expression (weighs against fair use)	Wrong answers are original new expression, but correct answers derived from the show totaled 643 (weighs against fair use)	The book was a derivative work, harmed potential market (weighs against fair use)	NOT FAIR USE
A designer scanned and digitally altered a photo for use in a multimedia work	Multimedia work was for commercial use (weighs against fair use)	The source photograph was creative expression (weighs against fair use)	The entire photograph was copied (weighs against fair use)	Multimedia work directly affected market (weighs against fair use)	NOT FAIR USE
Search engine displayed photo search results as thumbnails	Search results are transformative — public benefit of search engine (weighs for fair use)	Photos are published creative works (weighs against fair use)	Entire photo used, but shown only as much as necessary (weighs for fair use)	Thumbnails did not harm market; led people to originals (weighs for fair use)	FAIR USE
Search engine displayed photo search results as thumbnails, which are also sold for cell phone downloads	Search results are transformative — public benefit of search engine (weighs for fair use)	Photos are published creative works (weighs against fair use)	Entire photo used, which constitutes the product (weighs against fair use)	Posting thumbnails in search results harms market for thumbnail downloads (weighs against fair use)	NOT FAIR USE? (ON APPEAL)

What about international copyright?

When working on Internet projects, you need to be aware of the international law that affects your ability to use materials and to protect your work. International copyright law is composed of the various treaties and conventions that countries around the world have chosen to adopt. However, these treaties do not allow you to simply register a work with a worldwide organization and gain protection; you still need to meet the requirements of the copyright law of a given country. For more information, visit the World Intellectual Property Organization at *www.wipo.org*.

But is my unauthorized use really wrong?

Whether you use material appropriately is a function of your ethics and values, and your comfort in taking risks. Whether you'll get caught if you infringe someone's copyright depends on many variables. When it comes to using protected work under fair use, we'd all like to think our use of copyright-protected work is fair, but that is not always the case.

■ Maybe I won't get caught

Many people base their actions on what they think their chance is of getting caught. Innocent and willful infringements occur thousands of times a day at colleges, universities, homes, and businesses. If the topic is illegal downloading and you've downloaded a total of 10 songs, it doesn't seem likely anyone would come after you. But bear in mind that the entertainment industry, through its groups the Motion Picture Association of America (MPAA) and the Recording Industry Association of America (RIAA), have established legal inroads and have enormous financial capacity to pursue individual infringers. The RIAA has sued more than 20,000 individuals and settled with 25 percent of them for an average of $3,600. If the issue centers on you using protected work improperly in a work you've created and the copyright owner becomes aware of your use (which is increasingly likely with digital watermarking and other identification technologies), you can prepare for legal action.

The entertainment industry has extensive resources that can be brought to bear in long, complex, and expensive cases.

■ I'm really not stealing much

It can be tempting to indulge in philosophical arguments about where copyright infringement ranks on the crime scale, but ultimately this is irrelevant. Comparing infringement to violent crimes such as murder is about as useful as comparing it to receiving a parking ticket. The issue is not about your subjective opinion of how harmful you think infringement is, but rather the investment the interested parties have in preserving their stakes and their power to protect them.

■ No one would come after little old me

Many people, especially students and artists, adhere to a flawed logic that says that because they don't have much in the way of financial assets, they really have nothing to lose, so it wouldn't be worth the time or effort for anyone to sue them. The logic is flawed because reality has proved differently. One consequence of losing a copyright suit would definitely be the destruction of your work; additional consequences could be even more painful.

The entertainment industry has extensive resources that can be brought to bear in long, complex, and expensive cases and a clear strategy to stem the deluge of infringement that directly affects their bottom line. They aggressively pursue any alleged infringer without regard to a fair use defense—or your bank balance. If you're sued, you could try to negotiate a better settlement or hire an attorney, but that also costs money and time. Defendants, especially individual consumers or fledgling artists, might not have the financial resources necessary to defend themselves in kind, as the following examples illustrate:

Toy manufacturer Mattel, maker of Barbie, frequently takes action to protect its copyright or trademark by suing just about anyone who uses or references Barbie. Mattel has sued:

■ The Danish pop group Aqua for its song "Barbie Girl," claiming the group defamed Barbie by referring to her as a "blonde bimbo." Partial lyrics are shown in **Figure 30**.

■ Artist Tom Forsythe, who photographed posed dolls in kitchen appliances and cookware in a photographic essay named *Foodchain Barbie*. Mattel claimed the work was not parody and that he used too many Barbie dolls in the photographs.

■ The Quebec barbeque restaurant chain Barbie's, alleging that customers would be confused and associate it with the doll.

Figure 30: Lyrics to Aqua's song, *Barbie Girl*

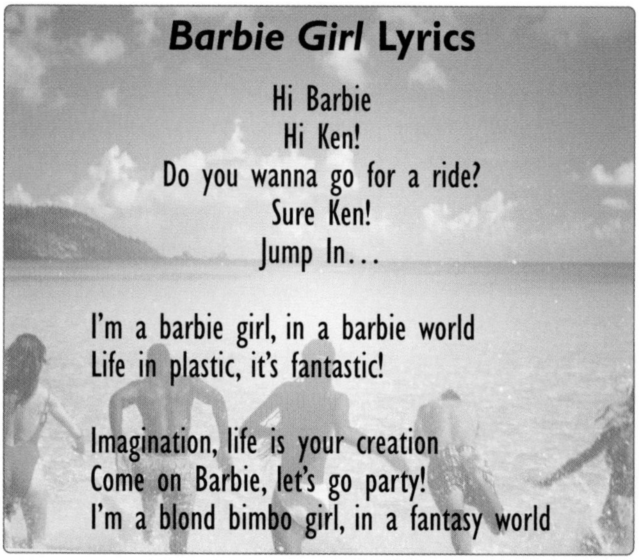

Barbie Girl **Lyrics**

Hi Barbie
Hi Ken!
Do you wanna go for a ride?
Sure Ken!
Jump In...

I'm a barbie girl, in a barbie world
Life in plastic, it's fantastic!

Imagination, life is your creation
Come on Barbie, let's go party!
I'm a blond bimbo girl, in a fantasy world

FYI

Many colleges are trying a new strategy to minimize illegal downloading by providing students a legal downloading service for free or for a minimal fee.

B UNIT

In each of these cases, the legal action went on for years, but in the end, each defendant prevailed when the court held that they did not infringe Mattel's copyright or trademark. The result in the Forsythe case is unusual and especially interesting because the court awarded him the cost of his legal fees, which totaled $1.8 million. In that ruling, the judge stated that "(p)laintiff *(Mattel)* had access to sophisticated counsel who could have determined that such a suit was objectively unreasonable and frivolous. Instead it appears plaintiff forced defendant into costly litigation to discourage him from using Barbie's image in his artwork. This is just the sort of situation in which this court should award attorneys fees to deter this type of litigation which contravenes the intent of the Copyright Act."

- In 1989, the Walt Disney Company discovered that three Florida daycare centers had painted large images of Mickey, Minnie, and Goofy on its walls. Disney threatened legal action if the centers did not paint over the images because the centers clearly violated Disney's copyright and trademarks. Upon hearing of the incident, representatives from rivals Hanna-Barbera and Universal Studios painted over the walls with images of Yogi Bear, Fred Flintstone, and Scooby Doo free of charge and rededicated the murals in a media event. Interestingly, in 2002, a medieval fresco was uncovered in the Austrian village of Malta that appears to show a 700-year-old image of Mickey Mouse, shown in **Figure 31**. The village has (jokingly) claimed copyright infringement by Disney.

Figure 31: Alleged "original" Mickey Mouse on Austrian fresco

Educational uses naturally allow for much greater leeway for using protected work; the very nature of education demands access. But one of the most pervasive myths about copyright is that as a student or instructor, you are free to use as much as you want of any work for as long as you want. Or, that if you alter a work more than some percentage—10 percent or 25 percent are most commonly cited—the new work will not infringe the original. Regrettably, that is not the case. Teachers, students, and school administrators should take special care to understand both the benefits and the limitations of educational fair use. Students and artists alike should understand the special realtionship between parody and copyrighted works.

Understanding educational fair use

Teachers have the benefit of laws that deal specifically with distance learning, copying material for class, and using multimedia. These laws specify that copying for classroom use should meet the criteria of brevity, spontaneity, and lack of cumulative effect. That is, due to the nature of teaching, the teacher does not copy a significant amount, does not have the time to plan ahead and seek permissions to use the work, and does not use the same materials over and over (for example, in the same class year after year). **Figure 32** shows the relevant guidelines for instructors and students who want to digitize analog images or to create multimedia work for classroom use, self-study, or remote instruction. These are proposed guidelines only—they have not been embraced and incorporated into legislative materials because the group that met to devise them was unable to reach consensus on many issues, particularly whether these guidelines would provide the minimum protection against a copyright infringement suit, known as a **safe harbor**. Note that these are only proposed minimums; fair use analysis might provide the right to use more of a work. But the most important aspect to

remember is that there is *no* single accepted blueprint for using parts or percentages of any work. You'll find that most educational institutions have their own guidelines for students and faculty to use that incorporate these guidelines and other rules. Regardless of the specifics, as a student you can always keep one copy of your creations for your personal portfolio—not published on a Web page.

Understanding parody

Works of parody are some of the most visible works created under the rubric of fair use. As an art form, parody has amused the public and annoyed those being parodied since the Ancient Greek and later Roman Empires. **Parody** is the copying or imitation of a work in a satirical or humorous manner. Note that a use would not qualify as a parody if the purpose is simply to get attention or avoid the time and effort necessary to create something original. In the United States, parody

Figure 32: Proposed multimedia guidelines for teachers and students

Media		Quantity
	Motion media	Up to 10% or 3 minutes, whichever is less
	Text Poetry	Up to 10% or 1000 words, whichever is less Single poet: up to 500 words/portions but not more than three poems Multiple poets: five excerpts or poems by different poets from one anthology
	Music, lyrics, & music video	Up to 10%, but not more 30 seconds from an individual work
	Illustrations & photographs	Single artist: up to 5 images Collection: up to 10% or 15 images, whichever is less
	Database & data table	Up to 10% or 2500 field entries, whichever is less

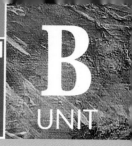
FYI

Performers such as Weird Al Yankovic, who earn a living by humorously modifying hit songs, seek permission of the songwriters before recording their parodies.

is closely associated with freedom of speech. Although parody is not specifically included in the Copyright Act, it became firmly established as a fair use defense to copyright infringement because of its obvious transformative qualities.

Parody's landmark case involved the 1994 recording of Roy Orbison's "Pretty Woman" by the rap group 2LiveCrew. Although the music was easily recognizable, the group changed the lyrics. The music company sued for copyright infringement.

The U.S. Supreme Court found that parody weighed heavily when considering the amount of copying and even the commercial nature of the work. You can compare the two songs by connecting to the Internet, navigating to the Online Companion, and then clicking Link 1, scrolling down to 1990–2000, clicking Acuff-Rose v. Campbell, then clicking the Hear Sound Recording link to listen to both versions. Sample lyrics from both songs are shown in **Figure 33**.

preclude it from being fair use. Specifically, parody as a derivative use is not considered harmful to the market for the copyright holder, although this view remains controversial. That is, although copyright owners have a right to the markets made available by a parody-based derivative use of the work, owners are not presumed to be the ones who would parody their own work, even though they certainly could.

But the most important aspect to remember is that there is *no* accepted blueprint for using parts or percentages of any work.

Figure 33: Comparing lyrics in the 2LiveCrew "Pretty Woman" parody case

Roy Orbison lyrics

Pretty woman, won't you pardon me
Pretty woman, I couldn't help but see
Pretty woman, and you look lovely as can be
Are you lonely just like me

2LiveCrew lyrics

Big hairy woman, you need to shave that stuff,
Big hairy woman, you know I bet it's tough.
Big hairy woman, all that hair ain't legit,
'Cause you look like Cousin It.

Significance: The ruling established that parody was an acceptable case of "transformative use." It also confirmed that a parody is fair use and the commercial value of the work does *not* automatically

Other cases soon followed that furthered parody as a fair use defense, including a parody of an Annie Lebovitz photograph of pregnant actress Demi Moore. A movie company advertised the film *Naked Gun 33 1/3* by superimposing the head of actor Leslie Nielsen onto another photograph that was similar to the Leibovitz photo. The courts ruled against fair use, however, for a movie poster that emulated the famous *New Yorker* magazine cover that showed a skewed view of geography from a New York City resident's perspective, and a book about the OJ Simpson trial that copied the style and illustrations from *The Cat in the Hat*, by Dr. Seuss.

Copyright in Context Innovation versus protection

The future of copyright law will continue to explore and redefine the competing legal interests of consumers of creative material and rights holders. There is no doubt that technological advances will shape the social and economic underpinnings of copyright protection. To better understand these effects, it is helpful to examine technological innovations and how they are so relevant and contentious to copyright law.

What was the significance of the major file-sharing cases?

File-sharing companies Napster and Grokster each were sued by the entertainment industry. Each case had major ramifications through the convergence of technological innovation and copyright protection.

The legalities pit the entertainment industry against the technology industry. The entertainment industry maintains that if you supply a product knowing that it is predominantly used for infringement, you are a contributory infringer. The technology industry contends that capability does not indicate intent nor is capability in and of itself unlawful. **Figure 34** compares Napster's and Grokster's file-sharing configurations, both of which rely on a **peer-to-peer network**; that is, each computer on the network can share its files with other computers on the network.

Napster: Songs were routed through Napster's central server, which directly connected a query from one individual to another individual user's computer. In allowing users to browse and share copyright-protected works through their own server, Napster's centralized indexing was proof that it could prevent illegal downloading and, hence, infringement. Napster went bankrupt, its brand and logo sold, and has since been repackaged to download only licensed music.

Grokster: Grokster maintained they were innocent of vicarious infringement because they did not store any files on their central servers, which meant they could not be held responsible for the acts of those who used their software. Instead, songs were indexed through individual users' computers—the query went from one computer to the next (a decentralized server). However, Grokster promoted its ability to infringe and openly courted former Napster users. The Supreme Court ruled that a person or company that promotes use of software that can infringe copyright is liable for the infringing acts of those who use the software. The case established inducement as an infringing act: Grokster induced others to use their software to infringe copyright. Grokster also went bankrupt and leaves a lasting message on its Web site, shown in **Figure 35**.

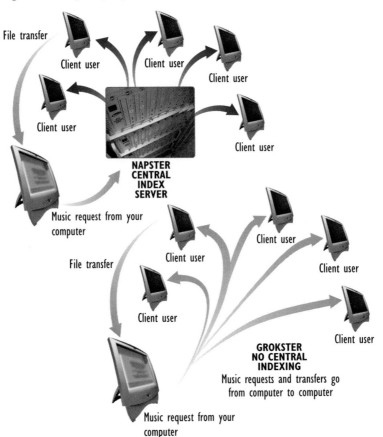

Figure 34: Comparing Napster and Grokster file-sharing

File transfer

Client user
Client user
Client user
Client user
Client user
Client user

NAPSTER CENTRAL INDEX SERVER

Music request from your computer

File transfer

Client user
Client user
Client user
Client user
Client user
Client user

GROKSTER NO CENTRAL INDEXING
Music requests and transfers go from computer to computer

Music request from your computer

Understanding the difference between copyright-free and royalty-free

A common but potentially confusing term is copyright-free. Americans tend to mistakenly equate it with works that are in the public domain, but this is not the case. Technically, copyright-free is the same as royalty-free. A royalty-free agreement means that a user can buy the right (license) to use a work on multiple occasions and for an unlimited amount of time. If you see a work identified as copyright-free, make sure to clarify its meaning with the owner of the work before you use the material.

Figure 35: Grokster's Web site after being shut down and going bankrupt

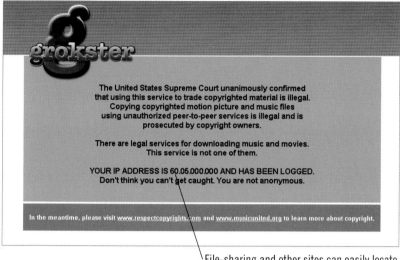

File-sharing and other sites can easily locate and store your computer's IP address

Similar arguments were used in shutting down BitTorrent, an effective file-sharing technology that was used to illegally download movies. In 2005, federal authorities (Homeland Security) shut down Elite Torrents' network users after thousands downloaded the prerelease of *Star Wars: Episode III*.

Understanding the Digital Millennium Copyright Act and digital rights management

The **Digital Millennium Copyright Act (DMCA)** penalizes anyone who attempts to circumvent (hack) anticopying technologies on digital media. DMCA made it unlawful to distribute or use such technology or devices. Under this law, you can excerpt sections from a written book under a fair use exception, but if you create software that circumvents anticopying measures on an e-book and then copy the same excerpts, you have violated the DMCA. Its critics question its constitutionality, specifically concerning reverse engineering and freedom of expression. The freedom of expression argument involves exposing critical technical weakness in a product or altering code for different purposes, such as the SONY Aibo robot dog enthusiast, who wrote code that made the toy jazz-dance, or the PlayStation fan who wrote code that allowed PlayStation games to be played on a PC. **Digital rights management (DRM)** is the technology that protects, restricts, and similarly controls access to digital media such as film, music, and software. The debate

around DRM exposes the legal stresses between protecting copyright and preventing competition.

Continue the conversation: Where do we go from here?

Colleges and universities are completely justified in dissuading copyright infringement, yet questions remain about whether they should offer up student identities in response to subpoenas from the entertainment industry. And, if the move to offer students access to legal download sites proves successful in reducing illegal downloads, should that discourage the push to ban file-sharing software?

Large corporations understandably have the right to protect their trademarks and copyrights. What does it say about our legal system that they correctly assume their financial resources will easily intimidate a legal opponent who uses a fair use defense?

As copyright protections increase, the public domain shrinks, which affects the exchange of ideas and society's ability to innovate by building on ideas.

Many see the law shifting emphasis toward copyright protection over public knowledge. These critics point out that as copyright protections increase, the public domain shrinks, which affects the exchange of ideas and the ability to innovate by building on ideas. Does society ultimately benefit by discouraging progress and innovation in favor of increased copyright protection?

On a positive note, many organizations seek new ground that supports technologies such as file-sharing software, while also supporting the compensation of copyright holders and the public's access to knowledge. To learn more about these organizations, visit the Electronic Frontier Foundation (*www.eff.org*) or the Chilling Effects Clearinghouse (*www.chillingeffects.org*).

End of Unit Exercises

Key Terms

Cease and desist letter

Contributory infringement

Copyright-free

Copyright infringement

Digital Millennium Copyright
Act (DMCA)

Digital rights management

Direct infringement

Fair use

Indirect infringement

Innocent infringement

Limitations

Parody

Peer-to-peer network

Plagiarism

Royalty-free agreement

Safe harbor

Substantial similarity

Transformative

Vicarious infringement

Willful infringement

Unit Review

1. Discuss whether you can use media at a site that does not include terms of use.

2. Give one reason why obtaining permission to use a multimedia work can be more complex than obtaining it for a single media work, such as a painting.

3. How does the burden of proof in a civil copyright infringement suit differ from the burden of proof in a criminal law?

4. Explain why attribution is good practice and yet not a defense to copyright infringement.

5. What is the difference between innocent infringement and willful infringement?

6. List three elements that are important to include in a permissions letter to a copyright holder.

7. Explain why only using a small amount of a protected work can still infringe the original.

8. Explain why even starving artists need to be concerned about being sued for copyright infringement if they use protected work in their life's masterpiece.

9. Discuss the difference between contributory infringement and vicarious infringement.

10. Explain how a transformative work might not infringe copyright.

Fill in the Best Answer

1. The primary limitation or exception to copyright protection is known as the _____ doctrine.

2. Vicarious infringement and contributory infringement are categories of _____ infringement.

3. The first sign that you have been discovered using copyright-protected work is when you receive a _____ letter.

4. Minimum guidelines that afford protection against a copyright infringement suit are known as providing a _____.

5. The 2LiveCrew recording of "Pretty Woman" established _____ as fair use.

6. The degree to which a work resembles a copyrighted work is known as _____.

7. Using the ideas and writings of others and representing them as your own is known as _____.

8. The fourth fair use factor, Effect, is weighted the highest by the courts because it relates to the _____ for the copyrighted work.

9. Quoting the punch lines of several jokes to analyze and compare humor in a paper is fair use because the material is _____.

10. The key or central portions of a work are known as the _____.

Select the Best Answer

1. As of this writing, the damages for willful infringement can be as high as:

   a. $1,000.

   b. $10,000.

   c. $100,000.

   d. $150,000.

2. Which of the following is *not* a requirement for proving copyright infringement?

   a. The infringer's new work has commercial value.

   b. The infringer copied the work.

   c. No permission was given to use the work.

   d. The work is protected by copyright.

3. If you are sued for copyright infringement, you are presumed:

   a. Innocent no matter what.

   b. Innocent if prima facie evidence is proved.

   c. Liable if prima facie evidence is proved.

   d. To have made money from your use.

4. In a multimedia piece, which of the following is the most likely to be difficult to obtain permission for?

   a. A small portion of a photo of a jellyfish downloaded from the Monterey Bay Aquarium.

   b. An entire recording of a hip-hop song about whales that includes actual whale songs.

   c. The sound of splashing water as a slide transition sound.

   d. The logo of the Monterey Bay Aquarium.

5. Your satirical skit about the mayor's new antilitter campaign has been a big hit at local events. However, the mayor has now expressly refused to give you permission to use the antilitter material in the skit and, furthermore, he said he doesn't think the skit is funny. Legally, what can you do?

   a. Hope he doesn't sue you for infringing his copyright for the antilitter material and that you've paid all your parking tickets.

   b. Hope he doesn't sue you for making money off of the skit and that you've paid all your parking tickets.

   c. Hope he doesn't sue you for inducing others to infringe his copyright and that you've paid all your parking tickets.

   d. Keep performing the skit because your work is a parody of both the mayor and the program, but make sure you've paid your parking tickets.

6. Registering your work with the Copyright Office allows you to:

   a. Negate any fair use argument on your work.

   b. Receive statutory damages if the infringer is found liable.

   c. Sue the infringer for pain and suffering you endured.

   d. Prevent any educational or multimedia use of your work.

7. Which of the following could be grounds for dismissing a copyright infringement suit?

   a. You used the protected work as the basis for creating a new work in a different medium.

   b. You downloaded the fewest songs of anyone you know and can prove it.

   c. You created the work independently and can prove it.

   d. You planned on asking permission but forgot.

8. Which of the following is the best-case scenario if you are found to be an innocent infringer by the court?

   a. You say "I'm Sorry" and walk away.

   b. You pay reduced damages decided by the court.

   c. You must locate and destroy every copy of the work that used the infringing material.

   d. You must pay royalties on thousands of copies of the infringing work.

9. Which of the following is usually not considered a part of multimedia work?

   a. Search results

   b. Music

   c. Voice-over

   d. Animation

10. Which of the following is considered a defense to copyright infringement?

   a. Ignorance

   b. Attribution

   c. Fair use

   d. Free advertising

End of Unit Exercises

INDEPENDENT CHALLENGE 1

You've created a Macromedia Flash game that tests how long it takes for a player to recognize a song. A player listens to several songs for 3 to 5 seconds, and then has 10 seconds to select the songs from a list. The theme from "Jeopardy" plays in the background while the player selects the songs.

Based on your knowledge of copyright, discuss the infringement implications for the following situations:

1. Which elements of the game are eligible to be protected by copyright?

2. Which elements, if any, are infringing someone's copyright? How would you remedy the infringement before someone notices?

3. You created the game for your portfolio as you apply for developer positions at gaming companies, and don't plan to distribute it.

4. You give the game as a gift to your friends, so you do not profit from the distribution.

5. You post the game download link on your Web site and talk about it in several blogs and chat rooms, but do not charge money for it.

INDEPENDENT CHALLENGE 2

You're creating a video DVD yearbook that you plan to sell online, and you want to include as many elements as possible that suggest memories of the previous year.

Discuss the copyright ramifications and infringement remedies for the following elements in the yearbook:

1. Popular songs in their entirety as background music throughout the video.

2. Snippets from popular TV and movies.

3. Snippets from major news events.

4. Video and photos you take around town.

5. The price of the DVD yearbook is $10, but there's a $2 discount for students.

6. Whether you credit the songs, films, and news sources at the end of the video.

7. Write a sample permissions letter for any material you think may require it.

INDEPENDENT CHALLENGE 3

You have written a satirical play using characters from L. Frank Baum's original *Wizard of Oz*, written from Toto the dog's perspective. The name of the play is *Toto Tells All*.

1. After the first performance at your local theater, you receive cease and desist letters from:

   a. The estate of L. Frank Baum, author (who wrote the book *The Wonderful Wizard of Oz* in 1900 and died in 1919), saying you've made a derivative work of his original work

   b. MGM Studios, producers and distributors of the 1939 film *The Wizard of Oz*, saying you've made a derivative work of their original work

   c. Gregory Maguire, the author of *Wicked: The Life and Times of the Wicked Witch of the West*, a book written from the perspective of the famous witch, saying you've made a derivative work of his original work

   What is your response to each cease and desist letter?

2. In your play, you include a scene where the cast sings the popular song, "Happy Birthday," to Toto. Is this infringement? Why or why not?

3. You scan or download several photos of famous dogs, such as Lassie and Beethoven, and then enlarge them to use in the play. Is this infringement? Why or why not?

4. You found corporate sponsors to underwrite the play so you wouldn't have to charge more than a nominal fee for the performance. Would sponsorship affect the status of your work as a parody? If so, how?

INDEPENDENT CHALLENGE 4

 To better understand how copyright infringement cases are decided, you decide to review actual infringement cases and assess the facts on your own, knowing that your opinion would never hold water legally. Log on to the Internet, listen or watch the clips as instructed, then read the legal arguments. As an extra challenge, do not read the rulings until after you make up your mind.

1. Navigate to the Online Companion, then click Link 1.

   a. Scroll down to 1990-2000, click *La Cienega v. ZZ Top*, and then listen to both versions. Did you find substantial similarity between the two pieces? (*Note*: This case was ultimately decided on technical legal point and not whether the two pieces were substantially similar.)

   b. Click *ZZ Top v. Chrysler Corp.*, and then click View Video Clip. Did you find substantial similarity between the two pieces?

   c. Compare your opinion with the legal arguments and rulings, and then state whether you agree or disagree.

2. Navigate to the Online Companion, then click Link 2.

   a. Read down through the Film Imitates Art paragraph, and then view the clip. Did you find substantial similarity between the two pieces?

   b. Compare your opinion with the legal arguments and rulings, and then state whether you agree or disagree.

3. Navigate to the Online Companion, then click Link 3 and Link 4.

   a. Compare the posters. Did you find substantial similarity between the two pieces?

   b. In this case, the courts found that the poster to the movie *Moscow on the Hudson* was substantially similar to a famous cover of the *New Yorker* (1976), Steinberg's humorous take on geography from the standpoint of a Manhattanite, "View of the World from Ninth Avenue."

End of Unit Exercises

You've created a new energy drink called Purple Haze and want to develop an advertising campaign. Assess whether the following situations constitute copyright infringement. State why or why not. (*Note*: "Purple Haze" is the title of a classic rock song written by the innovative rock musician Jimi Hendrix.) Use the prototype shown in **Figure 36** as a reference.

Figure 36

Purple haze all in my brain
Lately, I don't feel the same

1. Can you name the drink Purple Haze? Why or why not?

2. Discuss whether lyrics from the song, as shown in the figure, can be used in any of the following:

   a. As a tag line in your advertising

   b. By a consumer magazine quoting the lyrics in a review of your product

   c. In a blog about great rock electric guitarists

3. Under which of the preceding circumstances, if any, would you need permission from the Hendrix estate, and why?

Glossary

Author The creator or owner of a copyrighted work.

Cease and desist letter Official written notification from a copyright owner that you have infringed the owner's copyright and that the owner demands you stop its use and distribution.

Contributory infringement When a person directly contributes to the infringement of someone's intellectual property.

Copyright An exclusive set of rights and legal protection granted to authors of original works, published or unpublished.

Copyright infringement Unauthorized use of copyrighted material that violates a copyright owner's exclusive rights.

Copyright-free Same as royalty-free; often incorrectly construed to mean in the public domain; a purchased license to use a copyright holder's work multiple times and for an unlimited amount of time.

Design patent Protects the overall ornamentative appearance of an object.

DMCA Digital Millennium Copyright Act; a bill that penalizes anyone who attempts to circumvent (hack) anticopying technologies on digital media.

Digital rights management The technology that protects, restricts, and similarly controls access to digital media such as film, music, and software.

Direct infringement When someone uses a copyrighted work without permission.

Fair use Allows limited use of copyrighted materials without permission of the copyright holder; the primary exception to copyright protection.

First sale doctrine A legal limit to a copyright owner's right of distribution; once a protected work has been sold for the first time, the purchaser can then redistribute the work without the author's permission.

Idea-Expression dichotomy Fundamental property of copyright law that protects the expression of an idea but not the underlying ideas or facts themselves.

Indirect infringement Infringement where you do not directly infringe a copyright, but you aid someone else's infringing conduct; two types of indirect infringement are contributory infringement and vicarious infringement.

Innocent infringement Use of a protected work where the infringer did not realize the work was protected.

Intangible asset An asset without physical substance.

Intellectual property A creative product of the human mind.

Intellectual property law Laws that protect intangible property such as creative expressions, inventions, slogans, and so on.

Limitations Exceptions to copyright law.

Merger doctrine A concept applied when there are very limited ways to express an idea, so the expression cannot be copyrighted.

Open access An adjunct to existing copyright law providing licensing that allows a copyright holder to retain certain rights to their work while generously releasing the work for others to use.

Original A product of the creator, although not necessarily novel or unique.

Parody The copying or imitation of a work in a satirical or humorous manner.

Patent law Legal protection of an invention, process, or method.

Peer-to-peer network A network comprised of multiple end-user computers rather than a designated server; used primarily for sharing files.

Plagiarism Falsely presenting someone else's work as your own.

Public domain Any work that no longer has copyright protection.

Right of privacy The right to be left alone and to be free from groundless publicity.

Right of publicity The right to control the commercial use of your identity.

Ripping The process of digitally extracting music or video from a CD or DVD to a computer.

Royalty Payment made to copyright holders for use of their work.

Glossary

Royalty-free agreement A purchased license to use a copyright holder's work multiple times and for an unlimited amount of time.

Safe harbor The minimum set or rules or regulations that will provide protection against a copyright infringement suit.

Scenes à faire Stock scenes, characters, and features of a work considered standard or essential to the genre or field.

Substantial similarity The degree to which a second work resembles the original copyrighted work.

Tangible medium of expression The material object in which a work can be experienced.

Terms of use The rules copyright owners set for use of their work.

Trade dress law Legal protection of the appearance and size of a product or service.

Trade secret law State-governed laws protecting secret formulas, recipes, or processes.

Trademark law Legal protection of an image, word, symbol, or design used to identify goods and services.

Transformative Work transformed by intangible input to be considered as fair use.

Vicarious infringement When a person or entity has direct control of the infringing activity and benefits financially from the infringement.

Willful infringement When the infringer uses a work and knows or should have known that the work was protected by copyright.

Work of authorship The categories of work that are afforded copyright protection.

Index

E

Electronic Frontier Foundation, 43

EULA (End License User Agreement), 14

F

fair use
    doctrine described, 34–35
    four factors of, 37
fan fiction, 16
file-sharing technology
    Grokster, Napster file-sharing cases, 42–43
    and vicarious infringement, 29
forms, copyright, 10, 11

G

Grokster file-sharing case, 42–43
guidelines for multimedia use, 40

I

ideas, and copyright protection, 2, 12
images on Web pages, 18, 40
infringement
    copyright. *See* copyright infringement
    described legally, 27
infringement suits, 10, 29
innovation, balancing with copyright protection,
    3, 42–43
intellectual property
categories of, 5
and copyright law, 3
described, 2
international copyright, 37
Internet
    downloading media, and copyright, 2–3, 40
    obtaining permission to use works from, 32–33
iPods, 9

L

lawsuits
    determination of fair use, 37
    file-sharing cases, 42–43
    infringement, 10, 26
    statutory damages, attorney's fees, 10
libraries, finding useable media, 14
licensing, music and royalties, 16
limitations, copyright, 26

M

Mattel, and infringement, 38–39
media
    copyrighting protected work into
        different, 35
    finding usable, 16–17
    multimedia permissions, 33, 40
merger doctrine, 12
Mickey Mouse, 38–39
Microsoft clip art, 14
Motion Picture Association of America (MPAA), 38
MP3 players, 9
multimedia permissions, 33, 40
museums, photographing art in, 19
music
    downloading, 9, 29, 42–43
    sampling, 7

N

Napster file-sharing case, 42–43

O

obtaining
    copyright forms, 10
    copyright protection, 4–7
    permission to use someone's work, 32–33
Orbison, Roy, 41